where TO

now?

Australia's Identity in the Nineties

Editor: J Beaumont

THE FEDERAION PRESS
1993

Acknowledgments:

An important contribution to this book has been made by the delegates to the 1993 Winter School Conference whose questions provoked discussion. Among many, not all of whose names were recorded, are: Lynn Arnold, Enid Davis, Beverley Fletcher, Barry Maley, Hugh Ralston and Lee Santow. The editor is indebted to them all and has incorporated questions where possible in the commentary sections.

The editor acknowledges with gratitude, the assistance of: Christine Baker; Roslyn Hunyor; Alistair Maclennan; Jennifer Maclennan; Rosemary Rule; Dr Judith Williams.

Reproduced by the kind permission of the publishers, Harper Collins:

"Night Sowing" by David Campbell from his *Selected Poems* 1942-68), A & R, 1968.
Extract from "Australia" by AD Hope from his *Collected Poems*, A & R, 1966.

Published in Sydney by

The Federation Press Pty Ltd
PO Box 45, Annandale, NSW, 2038.
3/56-72 John St, Leichhardt, NSW, 2040.
Ph (02) 552 2200; Fax (02) 552 1681.

National Library of Australia cataloguing-in-publication

Where to now? : Australia's identity in the nineties.

Includes index
ISBN 1 86287 124 8

1. Australia. Constitution. 2. Pluralism (Social sciences) - Australia. 3. Australia - Civilization - 1990- . 4. Australia - Civilization - Philosophy. 5. Australia - Relations - Asia. 6. Asia - Relations - Australia. I. Beaumont, J. (Jeanette).

994.063

© The Federation Press

First published 1993

This publication is copyright. Other than for the purposes of and subject to the conditions prescribed under the Copyright Act, no part of it may in any form or by any means (electronic, mechanical, microcopying, photocopying, recording or otherwise) be reproduced, stored in a retrieval system or transmitted without prior written permission. Enquiries should be addressed to the publishers.

Typeset by The Federation Press, Leichhardt, NSW.
Printed and bound by Southwood Press Pty Ltd, Marrickville, NSW.

FOREWORD

Ann Eyland

This book arose from a Winter School held at The Women's College within the University of Sydney on July 17 and 18 1993. The Winter Schools have been organised by former students of the College and have their genesis in the Centenary Summer School of 1989 which celebrated one hundred years since the passing of the Act of Parliament which established the College.

Through its Winter Schools, the College celebrates its graduates and seeks to enhance their lives by providing a forum where the ideas and challenges of modern life can be explored. This year's theme, *Identity and Change — Australia in the 1990s*, was chosen early in 1992. I wish to acknowledge Jeanette Beaumont's prescience in choosing the theme, her inventiveness in developing it into such an exciting program and her courteousness which brought to the College the authors whose work fills these pages. The College was greatly honoured that such eminent Australians gave their time so generously and so effectively to provide a stimulating week-end. A number of those who contributed are graduates or former tutors of the College — Marie Bashir, Devleena Ghosh, Robin Marsden, Christine Dobbin, Sakuko Matsui, Jacqueline Menzies, and Jillian Oppenheimer. We were glad to be able to celebrate their work in such a forum.

The success of the Winter School led to requests for copies of the talks and so this book came into being. I wish to thank Chris Holt and Liz Halley from Federation Press for supporting the project and for making it possible to publish in such a short space of time. And of course the authors themselves who have responded very quickly to editorial requests so that publication deadlines could be kept. When they agreed to participate in the Winter School, they did not know that the task of preparing their papers for publication would be required. Without their ideas, and their co-operation, none of this would have happened. I thank them very much indeed.

Ann Eyland
Principal, The Women's College
University of Sydney
September, 1993

CONTENTS

Foreword — *Ann Eyland*	iii
Preface — *Brian Fletcher*	vii
Contributing Authors	x
I IDENTITY AND CHANGE	**1**
Introduction — *Brian Fletcher*	3
A National Movement that Includes Us All — *Thomas Keneally*	5
A National Identity? Wait and See — *Hugh Mackay*	12
Commentary	26
II VOICES FROM MULTICULTURAL AUSTRALIA	**31**
Introduction — *Jeanette Beaumont*	33
Allegiance to a Community: Allegiance to a Country — *Jillian Oppenheimer*	35
Japan or Australia? Choosing Where to Live — *Sakuko Matsui*	37
The Losses and Gains of Living in Another Country — *Devleena Ghosh*	39
The National Debate Threatens Social Structures — *John Berwick*	41
An Organic and Diverse National Identity — *Andrew Riemer*	45
Commentary	48

CONTENTS

III THE CONSTITUTION	53
Introduction	
— *Margaret Beazley*	55
Origins of the Australian Constitution	
— *Margaret Beazley*	57
What the Constitution Says	
— *Sir Maurice Byers*	60
Is Change Recommended?	
— *Sir Maurice Byers and Sir Harry Gibbs*	67
Commentary	79
IV BRAVE NEW REPUBLIC	83
Introduction	
— *Kim Santow*	85
A Republican Model: Would More be Better than Less?	
Cheryl Saunders	86
Some Remarks about the Republic	
Roger Gyles	97
Commentary	102
V IDENTIFYING WITH ASIA	111
Introduction	
— *Pamela Gutman*	113
An Australian Presence in Asia? An Australia Foundation?	
— *Alison Broinowski*	115
Australian-Asian Perceptions	
— *Anthony Milner*	122
Commentary	133
VI DIPLOMATIC AND POLITICAL TIES WITH ASIA	137
Introduction	
— *Christine Dobbin*	139
A Journey through Australia's Regional Diplomacy	
— *Tim McDonald*	141
Regional Relations: The Politics of Continuing Change	
— *Rodney Tiffen*	152
Commentary	157

CONTENTS

VII AUSTRALIAN AND ASIAN LITERATURE — 167

Introduction
— *Robin Marsden* — 169

Asia in the Australian Literary Imagination
— *Yasmine Gooneratne* — 171

Some Thoughts on Asian Studies
— *Pierre Ryckmans* — 182

Commentary — 187

VIII AUSTRALIAN ARTISTS AND ASIA — 189

Introduction
— *Marie Bashir* — 191

From Orientalism to Interchange —
Australian Artists to Asia 1870s-1990s
— *Jacqueline Menzies* — 192

Endnotes — 206

Index — 211

PREFACE

Brian Fletcher

More, perhaps, than at any previous stage of its history, Australia is currently confronted by a multiplicity of problems that strike at the root of much that was once taken for granted. These problems need lengthy, careful public debate of a kind to which there is a need to become more accustomed. There are no quick solutions. What is required is for informed opinions from a range of experts to be put forward so that they can be given serious consideration.

This, fundamentally, is the aim of the present book., which is the outcome of a conference that was held at the Women's College in the University of Sydney on 17 and 18 July 1993. The papers and accompanying discussion are presented in edited form, and they deal with a theme of great contemporary importance, namely that of identity and change in the Australia of the 1990s.

A wide range of Australians prominent in numerous spheres of life have contributed to this book. They include distinguished legal figures, literary celebrities, leading public servants, and academics drawn from a variety of disciplines, including history, sociology, political science and linguistics. Women are well represented, as are others whose background reflects the racial and ethnic diversity of modern Australia. There is also a blend of political opinions stretching across the spectrum from left to right. The result is a volume that covers a wide range of opinions, thus providing an opportunity to view the issues discussed from a number of different standpoints.

Indeed, among the strengths of this book is the fact that it avoids the glib answer and the oversimplified response. It well reflects the present state of a society that is currently engaged in the task of rediscovering itself. This is a phenomenon that is by no means peculiar to Australia. Other nations are also looking again at their identity and making adjustments in the light of changed circumstances. Some, like Japan, find themselves in situations where their economic wealth and world standing have improved dramatically. Others, like Britain, are confronted with the need to adjust to the reverse of this process. Whereas Britain has become a post-imperial power, Australia is one of a number of post-colonial societies that are currently subject to a variety of new pressures.

The first chapters of the book look at what is occurring within Australia so far as a sense of identity, the nature of society and the future of the Federal Constitution are concerned. The picture that emerges confirms the fact that the community is experiencing a major transformation. Family life, as that concept was once understood, has changed dramatically in character. Women have come to play a new role in national life. Unemployment, much of it structural and in all likelihood permanent, has created new insecurities. Few would deny the existence of such realities, but differences of opinion are evident over questions such as the nature of national identity and whether conscious attempts should be made to impose such an identity. Similar divergences become evident when the republican issue is raised. Some either oppose the idea of constitutional change or warn of the need to tread carefully. Others view a republic as an historical necessity, a logical outcome of the whole course of development from the early days and a means of safeguarding ideals of social justice and racial equality. In all this, lies a basis for healthy and constructive discussion and for an interchange of differing views.

Besides exploring matters of domestic concern, this book also looks outwards, and in doing so touches a subject that has become intertwined with the republican debate. This is the relationship with Asia, which some see as destined to grow closer once Australia has freed itself from the last of its formal links with Britain. Constitutional change of this kind, it has been claimed, is a prerequisite for the strengthening of regional ties. Not everyone agrees and even some republicans have expressed doubts as to whether attitudes in Asia towards Australia have been greatly influenced by the existence of constitutional ties with the monarchy. Indeed, as Pierre Ryckmans points out, the term "Asian" is a western construct that encompasses so wide a variety of cultures as to be meaningless. What is made clear, however, is that diplomatic and trade links with the principal parts of this region have strengthened. Moreover,

PREFACE

migration to Australia from Asia has increased in volume since the decision was taken to end the White Australia Policy. Its abandonment, together with official and community rejection of the racist attitudes which underlay it, removed a longstanding source of friction and misunderstanding. Such developments point to major shifts in Australia's sense of national identity which, for a long time was based on notions of white superiority.

Further moves in this direction are obviously essential if Australia is to be more fully accepted into partnership by the nations of Asia. How this might be achieved forms a theme linking several of the chapters in this volume. The image of Asia, it has been argued, has been too strongly shaped by traditions deriving from Britain and Europe. One important message is the desirability for Asian society and culture to be viewed on its own terms and not through western eyes. If this goal is to be attained fresh approaches must be made to the way in which the subject of Asia is taught, particularly at school. Greater attention to Asian languages is also highly desirable. Positive steps that have already been taken were examined at the conference, but it was clear that more needs to be done. At the same time, if a meaningful dialogue is to take place, Australia must act to explain itself more fully to those whose friendship it seeks to enjoy.

Such a stark outline scarcely does justice to the subtle, sensitive and often sophisticated arguments that are presented in this book. Although by no means all questions are answered, it stands out as a positive, constructive volume that challenges existing stereotypes and offers suggestions for tackling some of the major issues that confront Australia in the 1990s. Fortunately there now exists a highly educated community, an increasing proportion of which has attended university. Such a situation increases the likelihood of a mature, reasoned response to the issues that need to be confronted during the remainder of the decade. The Women's College deserves gratitude for providing the forum for so seminal a conference, the outcome of which deserves serious consideration by all who are concerned with the future of Australia.

CONTRIBUTING AUTHORS

Brian Fletcher BA, DipEd, MA, PhD, FRAHS

Bicentennial Professor of Australian History at The University of Sydney since 1987, former Vice-President of Royal Australian Historical Society, co-editor *Journal of the Royal Australian Historical Society*. Publications include *Colonial Australia Before 1850*; *Ralph Darling A Governor Maligned History & Social Change*; *The GA Wood Memorial Lectures 1991* (editor), and *Australian History in NSW 1888-1938*.

Thomas Keneally, AO, FRSL, FAAAS, DLit (Hons) (Qld Uni)

Author; winner of many literary awards including The Booker Prize, The Miles Franklin Award, Commonwealth Literary Fund Fellowship, Los Angeles Times Fiction Prize etc. Visiting Professor at University of New York, University of California; President Australian Society of Authors; member of advisory panel on Individual and Democratic Rights Constitutional Commission; Chairman, The Australian Republican Movement. Works include *The Chant of Jimmie Blacksmith*, *Gossip from the Forest*, *Season in Purgatory*, *Schindler's Ark*, *The Place Where Souls Are Born* etc.

Hugh Mackay BA, FAPSS, FAIM

Psychologist and Social Researcher who has spent over 35 years studying the attitudes and behaviour of the Australian community. Chairman of Mackay Research; founder and director of The Centre for Communication Studies. Foundation member of the Board of Management of the St James Ethics Centre, a trustee of Sydney Grammar School and an honorary Professorial Fellow in the Graduate School of Management of Macquarie University. His book on the impact of social change, *Reinventing Australia* was published by Angus & Robertson in February 1993.

Andrew Riemer PhD, Lond, BA

Writer, literary critic and member of the Department of English at the University of Sydney. He is the author of several books on Shakespeare and Literary Editor of the *Independent Monthly*, as well as regular reviewer of books for the *Sydney Morning Herald* and the *Age* in Melbourne. *Inside Outside*, the story of his experience of life between two worlds, the old order in Europe and the new in Australia, received several literary awards in 1992. *The Habsburg Café* was published in 1993.

CONTRIBUTING AUTHORS

Jillian Oppenheimer BA (Syd) MA Hons (UNE)

Author *An Australian Clan: The Nivisons of New England*. Her family has been on the land for generations in the North of NSW. She has lectured in and researched regional history at the University of New England. Interested in history, heritage and conservation, she is deputy president of the National Trust. Former resident at the Women's College.

Sakuko Matsui BA, Konan, PhD

Associate Professor of Japanese, University of Sydney. Resident tutor The Women's College 1961-1971. 1st native born Japanese lecturer appointed to an Australian university after World War II. Author of *Natsume Soseki as a Critic of English Literature*, a study of one of Japan's first novelists. Translates for the University of Sydney East Asia Series, established 1987 to publish works on the history, literature, art and thought of China, Japan and Korea.

Devleena Ghosh B Ecs (New Delhi) MA Hons (Jadavpur)

Lecturer in Hindi at the University of Sydney; Resident at The Women's College 1984-1985. Educated Universities of Delhi (BEcs) and Jadavpur (MA Hons). Research interests: popular culture, women's studies, literacy and women's movements in India. Published numerous translations from Hindi, French and English into Bengali.

John Berwick BA (Hons), PhD (Syd), Dip Law

Barrister of the Supreme Court of NSW. Pacific correspondent *Telegraph* Calcutta (1991). Doctorate in Indian History. Research interests: modern Indian history, role of education in social change and law in South Asia.

Justice Margaret Beazley LLB (Hons)

Judge of the Federal Court of Australia; Queen's Counsel 1989; member of National Executive Amnesty International; Judicial Member of Equal Opportunity Tribunal; Chairperson Bar Council Law Reform Committee (1991).

Sir Maurice Byers Kt, CBE, QC

Solicitor General of Australia 1973-1983; Chairman Australian Constitutional Commission 1985-1988; leader Australian Delegation to UN Commission on international trade law, 1974-1982; past President NSW Bar Association.

Sir Harry Gibbs PC, GCMG, AC, KBE, BA, LLM

Hon LLD University of Queensland; Hon D Univ Griffith University; Chief Justice of Australia 1981-1987; Chairman Head of the Review into Commonwealth Criminal Law 1987-1991.

CONTRIBUTING AUTHORS

Justice Kim Santow OAM, BA, LLM,

Judge of Supreme Court of NSW. Part-time lecturer Master of Laws programme University of Sydney; author of a number of articles in law journals, trustee of the Art Gallery of NSW and of Sydney Grammar School; formerly trustee of Sydney Opera House.

Cheryl Saunders BA, LLB, PhD (Melb)

Director of the Centre for Comparative Constitutional Studies; holds a personal chair at the University of Melbourne Law School. Recently retired as the Chair of the Administrative Review Council; Deputy Chair of the Constitutional Centenary Foundation Inc.

Roger Gyles, QC, BA LLB

Barrister; Past President of Australian and NSW Bar Associations; Special Prosecutor of the Commonwealth 1982-1984; formerly Visiting Fellow of the University of Papua New Guinea; member of the Administrative Review Council; Royal Commissioner, Productivity Building Industry.

Pamela Gutman BA PhD (ANU)

Deputy Director of the Research Institute for Asia and the Pacific at the University of Sydney. After completing her doctorate in Asian Studies at the Australian National University she joined the Department of Immigration and Ethnic Affairs, where she worked on refugee policy, ethnic affairs and control, and was Executive Assistant to the Secretary. As a senior officer in the Foreign Affairs Branch of the Department of the Prime Minister and Cabinet she had responsibility for Asia and other regions, and in 1988 joined Professor Ross Garnaut in the preparation of his report to the Prime Minister and the Minister for Foreign Affairs and Trade, *Australia and the Northeast Asian Ascendancy*.

She has published widely in Australia on Asian affairs, and is a member of the Australia in Asia Council, the Pacific Economic Cooperation Council Human Resource Development Working Group, Vice-President of the Asian Studies Association of Australia and coordinator of the Research Institute for Asia and the Pacific's national lead institution function for the Asia Pacific Economic Cooperation Human Resource Development Business Management Network. She recently co-authored Global Population Movements and their Implication for Australia (AGPS Canberra 1993).

Alison Broinowski BA (Adelaide)

Writer and Australian diplomat; spent 15 years in Japan, Burma, Iran, The Philippines, South Korea, Jordan and the USA. She is a well known reviewer and broadcaster; has published 3 books on South East Asia. *The Yellow Lady — Australian Impressions of Asia* published in 1992 has already been reprinted in paperback. Broadcaster, reviewer, Chair of Melbourne Writers' Festival.

CONTRIBUTING AUTHORS

Anthony Milner BA (Monash), MA, PhD (Cornell)

Director of the Australian-Asian Perceptions Project of the Academy of Social Sciences in Australia, and Reader in History at the Australian National University. He is a South East Asian specialist and has written widely on Malay history. His most recent book "The Invention of Politics" will be published by Cambridge University Press in 1994.

Robin Marsden BA Hons (Syd)

Hon associate editor of *Quadrant*; literary editor of *The Australian Quarterly* 1957-1961; former undergraduate student then tutor English at The Women's College 1957-1961; currently on the staff of a publishing firm, CCH Australia

Pierre Ryckmans LLD PhD FAHA

Writer and academic; professor of Chinese at the University of Sydney. Has given courses in art history at the Chinese University of Hong Kong and served as cultural attache at the Belgian Embassy in Peking. Writes under the pseudonym Simon Leys and has won various literary awards. Has published seven volumes of translations from the Chinese as well as works of his own on Chinese, and other subjects. *Chinese Shadows* is regarded as a masterpiece. *Death of Napoleon* received the Christina Stead Critics Award, and in the UK, *The Independent's* 1992 Best Foreign Fiction of the Year award.

Yasmine Gooneratne AO, BA Hons (Ceylon), PhD (Cambridge), DLitt (Macquarie)

Academic, poet, essayist, critic and novelist. She holds a Personal Chair in English Literature at Macquarie University, where she is also Foundation Director of the Postcolonial Literatures and Language Research Centre, established in 1988. Her publications include *English Literature in Ceylon 1815-1878* (Dehiwela 1968), *Jane Austen* (Cambridge 1970), *Alexander Pope* (Cambridge 1976), *Relative Merits, — A Personal Memoir of the Bandaranaike Family of Sri Lanka* (London and New York 1986), four volumes of poetry, *Diverse Inheritance* (Adelaide 1980), *Silence, Exile and Cunning: The Fiction of Ruth Prawer Jhabvala* (Delhi 1983), and *A Change of Skies*, a novel which won the Marjorie Barnard Award for Fiction in 1992. She is Patron of the Jane Austen Society of Australia, Vice-President of the Federation Internationale des Litteratures et Langues Modernes (FILLM), and External Advisor to the English Department of the University of the South Pacific.

Christine Dobbin BA Hons (Syd), B Phil (Oxon), D Phil (Oxon)

Historian and officer of the Department of the Prime Minister and Cabinet. Has published three books, one translated into Indonesian. Has lectured widely in Australia and in Europe in South & South East Asian History. Fellow in Residence at the Netherland Institute for Advanced Study in 1988-1989 and for three years, member of The Australian Research Council's Asia Priority Panel.

CONTRIBUTING AUTHORS

Tim McDonald BSc, BEd (Melb)

Director, Research Institute for Asia and the Pacific, the University of Sydney. Former head of Administrative Division of Department of Foreign Affairs and Director of Aid Policy and Projects. Former diplomat in Asia Pacific Region — Deputy High Commissioner India, High Commissioner Bangladesh and Singapore, Minister and Deputy Chief of Mission, Australian Embassy Washington DC.

Rodney Tiffen BA, PhD (Monash)

Associate Professor, Department of Government and Public Administration, University of Sydney. Is a recognised expert on the relations of media and government both within Australia and in South East Asia. Adviser on media relations in Asia. His research and publications include *News from South East Asia: News and Power:* and co-editor of *Australia's Gulf War*.

Marie Bashir, AO, MBBS, FRANZCP

Clinical Professor of Psychiatry at the University of Sydney. Was a resident medical student at The Women's College 1950-1955 and the immediate past chairperson of its Council. Director of Community Health Services, Central Sydney area. She has studied the effects of dislocation and resettlement of refugee children in Laos, Cambodia, Vietnam and the refuge camps of South East Asia.

Jackie Menzies MA Syd (Oriental Studies)

Appointed first Curator of Asian Art at the Art Gallery of New South Wales in 1980, Jacqueline has been responsible for the development of the permanent Asian collections at the Gallery and their display in the specially designed Asian Gallery opened in 1990. She has initiated many exhibitions on Asian art and is the author of many catalogues and articles. While her particular interest in Asia is the arts of China, Korea and Japan, she has a related interest in cross-cultural exchange between Australia and Asian cultures, and curated the first exhibitions to examine the impact of Asian cultures on Australian artists.

I
IDENTITY AND CHANGE

INTRODUCTION

Brian Fletcher

The present decade is widely believed to possess special significance for Australia. Leading political figures and journalists have consistently endeavoured to arouse expectations of new and exciting developments calculated to breathe fresh life into the nation and equip it for the challenge of the coming century. Such attitudes are by no means confined to Australia. In other countries too, the closing years of the century have come to be viewed as providing opportunities for stocktaking and fresh initiatives. Local commentators, however, have been able to draw on precedents unique to Australia when presenting their forecasts. A century ago, a succession of events occurred that helped to remould attitudes and reshape institutions. The 1890s opened with the worst depression to strike the Australian colonies. Confidence was undermined and doubts arose as to whether the label "land of opportunity" was any longer applicable. The depression was accompanied by industrial disputes of a magnitude not earlier experienced and class divisions, hitherto submerged, were brought to the surface. These divisions were given additional potency by the formation of Labor Parties in the various colonies. This greatly altered the face of politics and gave further stimulus to the emergence of the welfare state. Developments such as these were of positive value and so too was the growth of national sentiment. Its emergence affected cultural as well as political life, contributing to the movement for Federation and the ultimate decision to form the Commonwealth of Australia. The significance of such developments and their relationship to what had occurred earlier, have been the subject of debate among historians. Cumulatively, however, these changes did make the 1890s the kind of turning-point that some present-day observers would like the 1990s to become.

Ironically enough, the expectations thus held out seemed in danger of being soured by an unwanted historical parallel between the two decades. The fall in commodity prices, the continuing balance of payments deficit and serious unemployment, have all contributed to a downturn in economic conditions that are only too reminiscent of the early 1890s. Fortunately this has not been allowed unduly to colour present-day thinking. All sides of the political spectrum appear to view economic setbacks more as a challenge to be overcome than as an insuperable obstacle. The prevailing mood remains positive and the hopes of creative change are still strong. Such attitudes were well reflected in the conference whose papers form the basis of the present book.

The issues addressed in the chapters which follow scarcely existed a century ago. Throughout the 1890s the Australian colonies, while conscious of being distinctive, remained secure in their attachment to the mother country. Nationalism, as it then existed, embodied feelings of patriotism as well as a pride in being British, "A man is none the less a good Australian because he is proud of his British origin and of the old blood", observed Sir Edmund Barton, Australia's first Prime Minister. National identity was for the most part taken for granted, as was the fact that it was male-oriented and white-centred. Nowadays, most of the assumptions that then underlay such convictions have been called into question by a multicultural society in which British influence has waned, in which gender relations have undergone fundamental modifications and in which attempts are being made to forge new relationships with the Aboriginal people and with the outside world. The task of appraising the process of "Identity and Change" during the current decade is rendered more complex and difficult by the many uncertainties that confront Australia. The situation is not made any easier by the decision of the Keating Government to press for the establishment of a republic by the turn of the century. This has created further divisions and has generated heated debate.

A National Movement that Includes Us All

Thomas Keneally

When I was a young writer, we were all considered Commonwealth writers. There are university departments of Commonwealth Literature all over the world, and one of the premises on which these departments are based is that there is a continuity between the experience of, say, Patrick White of Australia, Wole Soyinka of Nigeria, and VS Naipaul of Trinidad. One of the aspects of continuity between all such Commonwealth writers, up to this point of history, was that we were raised with a sense that we were out on the periphery. The sense that there was a centre — Europe — where everything was done essentially better than we could do it, whether it was a matter of dining, of vowels, or of cultural sensibility.

I think the difference between my generation and the rising generation of the present is that young Australians now, while not for a second denying the importance of European heritage, have ceased to consider Europe the absolute centre.

It must be all the harder for them then to understand that in early European Australia it was difficult for the European sensibility to find a purchase, a spiritual home in Australia's wantonly anti-European strangeness. Sometimes, finding no handhold, no European template, people gave up in disgust. The first Lieutenant Governor of New South Wales, who was a moaning Scot named

Major Robert Ross, comes up in the midst of a whingeing letter back home to Undersecretary Nepean, with a remarkable and passionate perception. "I do not scruple to pronounce", he writes, "that in the whole world there is not a worse country than we have yet seen of this. All that is contiguous to us is so very barren and forbidding that it may with truth be said — here nature is reversed . . ."[1]

You can feel with Robbie that, struggling for expression in his tent, he still cannot get out how weird the damn place is. And yet — on the other hand — he is in Sydney Harbour, tourist dream of the late 20th century.

Many European observers were defeated by Australia. Barron Field, early judge of the Supreme Court and poet, complained that poetry was impossible here in Australia.

> The common consent and immemorial custom of European poetry has made the change of the seasons, and its effect upon vegetation, a part of our very nature. I can therefore hold no fellowship with Australian foliage.[2]

He also wonders whether Australia has the same theological standing as the rest of creation:

> Kangaroo, Kangaroo!
> Thou spirit of Australia
> That redeems from utter failure,
> From perfect desolation,
> And warrants of the creation
> Of this fifth part of the Earth,
> Which would seem an afterbirth,
> Not conceiv'd in the Beginning
> (For God blessed His work at first
> And saw that it was good),
> But emerg'd at the first sinning,
> When the ground was therefore curst;
> And hence this barren wood![3]

The tone of this passionate alienation of this bitter poem about Australia written in 1819, turns up nearly a 120 years later in AD Hope's more loving poem, "Australia". Australia is described here as:

> The last of lands, the emptiest,
> A woman beyond her change of life, a breast
> Still tender but within the womb is dry.[4]

A NATIONAL MOVEMENT THAT INCLUDES US ALL

Alec Hope's perception accorded with that of DH Lawrence, during his visit to Australia in 1922. In *Kangaroo*,[5] you can find the same denials, the same sense of failing to get an answer as in Barron Field.

> 'Como' said the station sign. And they ran on bridges over two arms of water from the sea ... a bit like Lake Como but oh, so unlike. That curious sombreness of Australia, the sense of oldness, with the forms all worn down low and blunt, squat ... the strange, as it were, invisible beauty of Australia, which is undeniably there, but which seems to lurk just beyond the range of our white vision. You feel you can't see — as if your eyes hadn't the vision in them to correspond with the outside landscape. For the landscape is so unimpressive, like a face with little or no features, a dark face. And yet, when you don't have the feeling of ugliness or monotony in landscape ... you get a sense of subtle, remote formless beauty more poignant than anything ever experienced before.[6]

When one of the English characters, Harriett, praises Australia: "Your wonderful Australia!", she then contradicts herself by saying:

> It feels as if no one had ever loved it. Do you know what I mean? England and Germany and Italy and Egypt and India — they've all been loved so passionately. But Australia feels as if it had never been loved, and never come out into the open. As if man had never loved it, and made it a happy country, a bride country — or a mother country...[7]

And then the Australian character, Jack, chimes in:

> I'm afraid most Australians come to hate the Australian earth a good bit before they're done with it. If you call the land a bride, she's the sort of bride not many of us are willing to tackle. She drinks your sweat and your blood, and then as often as not lets you down, does you in...[8]

Patrick McCaughey, the Australian curator of the Hartford Athaneum, gave a lecture at Yale in which he argued that Sidney Nolan and Russell Drysdale painted Australians, often solitary males, as Orpheus descended into the Underworld. So that although Nolan and White ended life as enemies, they both (in Nolan's *Burke and Wills* and in White's *Voss*[9]) depicted the European as a fated lost figure in a landscape, a landscape that needed their sacrifice to give it meaning. Australia was a purgatory and vacancy for sensitive souls.

And so, although there were many Australians who never felt a sense of exile here, there was an age of exile, in which our major painters and writers felt somehow alien within Australia.

IDENTITY AND CHANGE

In my generation there have been many painters and writers who have taken to celebrating Australia — Fred Williams, Brett Whiteley, John Olsen; the poets Judith Wright and Les Murray. Other writers still, David Malouf, Elizabeth Jolley and Frank Moorehouse do not even address the question of whether Australia is heaven or hell, home or exile. They have grown out of the question.

Now the real questions can be asked — the questions which await us now that we have recovered as a society and culture from a sense of exile. You might not have as secure a promise of a job as, say, the young graduand AD Hope, but you have a securer sense of where you are and what it means.

The English language in Australia has undergone a transmutation as we began mentally to adjust ourselves to the continent. And the more the language was adjusted to Australian reality, the more Australian writers and Australian English speakers could achieve what Barron Field, in his diary, said was impossible — "A fellowship with Australian foliage".

The Canberra poet, David Campbell, wrote:

> Oh gentle, gentle land,
> Where the green ear shall grow,
> Now you are edged with light;
> The moon has crisped the fallow,
> The furrows run with night.
> This is the season's hour;
> While couples are in bed,
> I sow the paddocks late,
> Scatter like sparks the seed
> And see the dark ignite.
> Oh gentle land, I sow
> The heart's living grain.
> Stars draw their harrows over,
> Dews send their melting rain,
> I meet you as a lover.[10]

So David Campbell, at least, like you, was at home. He had his fellowship with the foliage.

The process of Australian culture has been to transfer our identity gradually away from the supposed "centre" (ie Europe) to the centre here. Australia, the outland and outlandish, slowly became the inland, the homeland, the focus of our imaginations.

In the way our literature and art mirrored that change, so did our constitutional development. Our Constitution was promulgated in Centennial Park on 1 January 1901, and it had a lot of the "centre", of Westminster, about it. It was largely the work of Australian politicians, but it was also filtered through the British Colonial Secretary and then finally passed as an Act of the Imperial British Parliament. To Australian patriots of the day, this was a reasonable arrangement. We depended upon the British for our institutions, our markets, and to protect us from intrusion by other nations. So it seemed appropriate that our Constitution did not echo any great drive for Australian sovereignty.

In the 1897 constitutional convention in Sydney, Edmond Barton said the Australian Government should not have any treaty-making power. That power "will be in the Imperial government". Sir George Reid hastened to agree with this. The "matter of treaties" is an expression which would be more in place in the United States' constitution where treaties are dealt with by the President and the Senate than in the constitution of a colony within an Empire". These two remarkable men, both of them future Prime Ministers, did not see the Constitution as giving Australia sovereignty.

Nor was the Governor-General to be an Australian institution. Before the Statute of Westminster in 1931, the Governor-General was appointed chiefly to look after Imperial interests in Australia. Our Australian Governments communicated with the Imperial Government at Westminster by way of the Governor-General of Australia and the Colonial Secretary of Great Britain. For example, in early 1907, Prime Minister Deakin wanted to find out from the French Government whether they intended to place political prisoners in New Caledonia. He asked the Governor-General to ask the Colonial Secretary to ask the Foreign Office to ask the British Ambassador in Paris to ask the French Foreign and Home Ministries. The message came back to Deakin from the French Government via the British Ambassador in Paris to the Foreign Office to the Colonial Secretary to the Governor-General to Alfred Deakin. Alfred Deakin asked the question in April 1907, and got the answer in July. Communications between the Australian Government and Westminster or Whitehall were not through the High Commissioner at Australia House, but again through the Governor-General and the Colonial Office.

Similarly, when the US Navy, the *Great White Fleet*, visited Sydney in 1908, Deakin was chastised for letting them into Sydney by Sir Edward Grey, the Foreign Secretary of the British Government. He told Deakin that "invitations to foreign governments should not be given except through us".[11]

Deakin went along with these arrangements not because he was wimpish or had colonial inferiorities, but because he envisaged a world in which Australia was a state within a potentially federated Empire. He believed that ultimately Australia and the Empire would make joint policy together, and this was a dream which entranced many Australian patriots, including Billy Hughes. Hughes regularly harangued the British Government about their habit of excluding Australia from peace treaties, noticeably from the treaty of Sevres, which put an end to the war between the Allies and Turkey. Billy Hughes certainly kicked up a fuss when the Turks burst down the Gallipoli Peninsula in 1922, having been provoked into it by Rumania and Greece.

> The habit of asking Australia to agree to things when they were done and cannot be undone and when there is only one course open to us in practice, and that is to support Britain — is one that will wreck the Empire if persisted in.[12]

If the Constitution was not intended to be the birth certificate of a fully sovereign and independent country, you nonetheless see throughout this century a gradual development of Australian sovereignty and independence. With the Statute of Westminster in 1931, the Governor-General became an Australian institution rather than a mere representative of British institutions. The Imperial Parliament also gave up virtually all its rights to make laws for us. Prime Minister James Scullin celebrated the fact by insisting that Isaac Isaacs, native born son of a Jewish haberdasher from Yackandandah, be made Governor-General. Towards the end of the 1930s we began to develop something like an independent diplomatic service, a tendency which became greater when Singapore fell in 1942. Gradually we cut out appeals to the Privy Council, the judicial committee of the British Cabinet. Appeals were finally abolished in 1986.

A NATIONAL MOVEMENT THAT INCLUDES US ALL

So as Australian writers throughout this century gradually centred their attention in Australia, so Australian sovereignty, became more and more located in Australia and not in the United Kingdom. I would argue that the final step of sovereignty, finding our own Head of State, without rancour or bitterness or denial, is inevitable. Others would argue that it is not inevitable, and I accept though do not agree with that sincerely expressed idea. But that Australia has become more of itself throughout this century and has become more of its region is something which cannot be denied.

And when I use the phrase "more of itself", I do not refer to 19th century nationalism. Nineteenth century nationalism existed to exclude others, to pretend to a divine destiny which other races did not share. Whatever the final form of government we resolve for ourselves throughout the decade, it will only work if it is inclusive. Whether it is a monarchy or a republic, it should not be like either the real monarchy or the envisaged republic of Australia in the 1890s. For Henry Lawson, though he extolled the young tree green of Australian fraternity over the old dead tree of the past and of sterile tradition, nonetheless sought to exclude many from his republic. He was particularly concerned to exclude Asians and Jews.

Our future state, republic or monarchy, will be worth nothing if it does not include, if it does not validate.

A National Identity? Wait and See...

Hugh Mackay

This is not a good time to be trying to define Australia's sense of its own national identity. On the other hand, it is a wonderful time to be exploring and debating the *question* of our national identity simply because, as we move into the 1990s, it is becoming clear that our social and cultural agenda is being dominated by issues which remind us that we are in the process of redefining the kind of society which we might become.

There have been times in the 20th century when Australia was said to have achieved a sense of nationhood which defined its identity: the time of Federation, in 1901, was such a period, and so were the years during and immediately after World War II. Both of those periods were characterised by commitment to a common purpose which evidently had a unifying and clarifying effect on our sense of who we were. Today, most of the significant social, cultural, technological, economic and political redefinitions which are taking place are having the opposite effect: far from unifying and clarifying our sense of identity, they have been fragmenting and confusing it.

Indeed, I think the best way to characterise Australians in the mid-1990s is to think of us as pioneers. We are living through a period in Australia's socio-cultural history when virtually all the conventions, the institutions, the landmarks and reference points which have traditionally been used for defining the Australian way of life have either disappeared, been challenged or redefined in some way. While we try to come to terms with such fundamental redefinitions and reinterpretation of Australian society, this is perhaps the moment to revive that outmoded and discredited term, "New Australian". Remember when we called immigrants "New Australians"? Remember when we thought that was a warm and welcoming label? Remember when we did not realise that it was potentially offensive to new arrivals (although I am not sure that it was ever more offensive than the term "ethnics" now in common use)?

Today, the term "New Australian" could be applied to all of us: we are all in the process of recreating the Australian way of life; we are all in the process of determining which institutions and conventions will define our culture. The only certainty is that yesterday's definitions will not work.

To appreciate the extent to which we are pioneering a new sense of national identity, it is only necessary to reflect upon some of the images which have traditionally dominated conventional descriptions of the Australian identity:

A MALE-DOMINATED SOCIETY?

A few years ago, I conducted a social research project in which I invited groups of Australians to reflect on what it means to be an Australian and to describe "typical Australians". A recurring theme in their discussions was that the typical Australian was masculine (and a bit of a larrikin).

Traditional images of the Australian identity have been dominated by masculinity. Today, when 51 percent of the population is female and when we are in the throes of a fundamental redefinition of gender roles, such imagery appears outrageous if not offensive.

If we want to take account of gender issues in our attempt to define our national identity, then we shall have to acknowledge that the contemporary gender role revolution may have precipitated some of the most significant and enduring redefinitions of Australian society.

I cannot think of a more fundamental shift in values than the shift which has resulted from the fact that women have utterly redefined their own role and status in our society. I cannot think of a more significant cultural revolution than the revolution brought about by women's rejection of second-class citizenship and second-hand identity.

Today it is merely absurd to speak of women as second-class citizens, or to consider that a woman would be defined by the presence or absence of a man in her life. But it is sobering to remind ourselves that it is not much more than 20 years since propositions like that were *generally* true of women in this society.

The women's movement has been a radical movement but, of course, its unifying proposition — "I am a person, determined to be treated in the same way as any other person" — only seemed radical because of the social and cultural context in which it emerged. What has been radical, undeniably, is the impact of that proposition on Australian women's view of themselves, their gender relations, their marriages, their families, and their work.

In other words, the gender role revolution, precipitated by women, is having a direct and sustained effect on many of those conventions and institutions by which a society defines itself.

The fact that women in Australia now have a particular view of gender roles which is still not widely shared by men has introduced new tensions into relations between the sexes and has, inevitably, redefined marriage. If we thought that the institution of marriage and the status of the family in our society would be defining characteristics of the Australian identity, then we had better wait and see how those institutions are going to evolve.

Twenty years ago, about 90 percent of our marriages were first marriages. Today, the figure is closer to 60 percent. Twenty years ago, one-third of all Australian women were married by the time they were 20. Today, the figure is 5 percent. The institution of marriage is being redefined.

The Institute of Family Studies estimates that about 25 percent of the rising generation of young Australians — those born in the 1960s and 1970s — will never marry. Between 35 percent and 40 percent of contemporary marriages will probably end in divorce, and that proportion is steadily increasing.

If these trends continue, it will be fairly safe to predict that, early in the 21st century, it will only be a minority of Australian adults who will marry once and stay married: the majority will contain those who never marry or marry two or more times.

In turn, this means that we are redefining the family. We have already accepted step-families, blended families, single-parent families, families based on de facto marriage relationships ... the term "the family" now embraces all these and other diverse and increasingly transient groupings.

If the family is being redefined, then so is the household. If we have at the core of our idea of national identity a cosy image of the Australian household as a place where the nuclear family dwells, we had better think again. Almost 50 percent of Australian households contain just one or two people. In our two major cities, Sydney and Melbourne, every third household contains just one adult — either a person living alone or a single parent. For that demographic reason, if for no other, loneliness is now a major social problem in our cities and the restructuring of the Australian household is leading to new patters of cooking and eating, new patterns of mass media consumption and will ultimately lead to new patterns of demand for urban housing as well.

Most of us would say that the family — however defined — is the social unit but, at a time when that social unit is in such disarray and when the institutions which define it are themselves being redefined, we will need to suspend judgement about this aspect of our national identity.

THE LAND OF OPPORTUNITY?

Traditional views of Australian society have characterised us as a land of opportunity where people who want to work hard can generally succeed and where, in spite of occasional economic downturns, future prosperity is more or less assured.

Today, such images sit very uncomfortably with our economic reality. Somewhere between one and two million Australians currently have either no work or much less work than they want.

Although we are getting used to the idea that unemployment is now likely to hover about 10 percent for the rest of the decade, we are still acting as though this is some kind of shock and as though high unemployment is a nasty — and unanticipated — economic accident.

But why are we shocked? Where did the sense of surprise come from? Unemployment hovered around 2.5 percent in the 1970s, it hovered around 5 percent in the 1980s (but reached 10 percent on at least one occasion) and was long predicted to reach present levels this decade — recession or no recession.

We are now beginning to acknowledge that, even when we begin to emerge from the recession, unemployment will not come down significantly. The term "jobless economic recovery" is now in the lexicon.

There are at least three factors which have been driving long-term unemployment, and we have embraced all three of them with enthusiasm:

- The massive participation of women in the labour market — in the wake of the women's movement — means that about 700,000 or 800,000 women now wish to participate in the work force whose mothers and grandmothers before them would not have wished to participate at the same point in the life cycle. The gender role revolution has fundamentally and irrevocably altered the relationship between the supply of work and the supply of labour.
- Micro-economic reform, leading to enhanced productivity, means that we are actively seeking ways of having the same amount of work done by fewer people, or more work being done by the same number of people. Micro-economic reform is very worthy from many points of view, but why does it surprise us that it is having a short-term negative impact on the supply of work?
- Technology — especially in the form of electronic information technology — is doing what it always promised to do: namely, replacing people by machines wherever possible. The defenders of technology tell us that short-term

loss of work in one area will lead to new industries springing up but, at least for the time being, that is no consolation.

For the foreseeable future, it looks as if we shall have to redefine the role of work in our society. Do we think that work is fundamental to the Australian ethic? Do we think that it is integral with the Australian sense of identity that everyone who wants work should have work? If we thought that were true, we would not have acted as we have acted in the past 20 years: if we thought that were true, we would have presumably looked at ways of redeploying available work so that those who wanted to share in the labour market were enabled to do so.

Increased use of part-time work — or generally shorter working hours — may sound like radical prescriptions, but they seem far less radical than the idea of paying more than one million of our citizens to stay at home and settle for no work at all.

Part of the Australian dream was that, one day, the Golden Age of Leisure would arrive, but is this it? Of course not. A situation in which people with full-time jobs complain of being over-worked and in which vast numbers of other people have no work at all is no "Golden Age" but an economic absurdity.

The small but growing number of Australians who have part-time work may be sending us a cheerful message from our future: they report that they lead a well-balanced life in which they have appropriate time and energy to devote to leisure and recreation and, accordingly, more energy to bring to their work. But there has been no massive and radical attempt to shift towards greater use of part-time work, simply because we have not yet come to terms with the possibility that work itself may have to be redefined.

If we were to redefine that place of work in our society, that would, in turn, involve us in restructuring our social security system — perhaps replacing our unemployment benefits with a range of top-up pensions for people with part-time work.

A redefinition of the place of work would also involve us in a fundamental rethink about the role of education: it is somewhat ironic that, at the very time when employment prospects for graduates are so dim, the emphasis in tertiary education continues to be on vocational training. (We hear that there are more lawyers-in-training than there are lawyers in Australia. Is that an example of poor educational planning, or are these student lawyers telling us something we need to know about our litigious future?)

For the time being, however, there are no signs that we are thinking about the long-term implications of sustained high unemployment. With further major retrenchments still being planned by corporate Australia, you would have to say that the Golden Age of Leisure is as far away as ever... and you would certainly have to say that, if Australians' attitudes to work are to be a significant dimension of our sense of national identity, then we had better wait and see what those attitudes will be.

THE EGALITARIAN SOCIETY?

A traditional view of Australia has been that this is an egalitarian society, dominated by a broad, comfortable middle class.

As in so many other departments of the Australian way of life, the 1990s find us pioneering new approaches to social class in Australia.

In the 20 years between the early 1970s and the early 1990s, the signs have been emerging that the egalitarian dream is over and that it is already offensive to large numbers of Australians to talk about Australia as a "middle-class" society.

In the past 20 years, we have so radically redistributed household income in Australia that we have created the framework for a new sense of social class. In that twenty-year period, households with a combined household income exceeding $72,000 per annum (in 1992 dollar terms) have doubled from 15 percent to 30 percent of Australian households. At the same time, households with a combined household income level of less than $22,000 per annum have increased from 20 percent to 30 percent of households.

You see what I am saying? Sixty percent of Australian households are either in that top or that bottom group. Where, then, is the dominant middle class? As in the United States, the Australian middle class has been shrinking steadily — down from 70 percent to about 40 percent of households in the past 20 years.

That top 30 percent of households now control about 55 percent of household income and the bottom 30 percent — exactly the same number of households — control about 10 percent of household income.

Of course, the impact of the women's movement is felt here, as in most other aspects of social, cultural and economic change in contemporary Australia. The ranks of the top-income households have been swelled by the phenomenon of the working mother: two-income households are now a mainstream economic phenomenon as about 60 percent of mothers of dependent children have full-time or part-time work outside the home.

Of course, not all of those working mothers are also wives: the ranks of the bottom 30 percent of households have also been swollen by the increasing phenomenon of single-parent families — generally families headed by a mother on a very low income. (In the Sydney suburb of Waterloo, for example, almost 50 percent of households are single-parent households and the vast majority of those parents are mothers.)

"Working mothers" are an important symbol of changing gender roles, changing patterns of marriage and family formation, and — most particularly — changing distribution of household income. Although many of those working mothers are sharing in the lives of very affluent, two-income households, others are fighting for economic survival at the bottom of the heap. They have seized their independence; seized the opportunity to escape, perhaps, from an unhappy or violent marriage; but they have also accelerated the process of redistributing household income.

It may well be objected that a mere redistribution of household income does not imply the creation of a new social class system. And yet, as history demonstrates, it is hard to see how such an unequal distribution of household income would not lead inexorably to an emerging new sense of social class.

For 20 years, we have been steadily creating a situation from which it may already be too late to retrieve ourselves: a situation in which the seeds of a new social class structure have already been sown.

It is almost certainly the case that wealthy Australians are already starting to feel superior to poor Australians. It is already the case that poor Australians are becoming aware of just how poor they are at a time when there is so much wealth flowing to others. As the rich become more protective of their wealth and the poor become increasingly angry about their poverty, it is hard to see how new urban tensions based on social class consciousness will be avoided.

Is the Australian identity to be defined by egalitarianism? We had better wait and see.

A FREEDOM-LOVING SOCIETY?

Whether justified or not, we have often tried to define the Australian character in terms of the value it places on freedom, and we have often entertained the idea that, by world standards, Australia is a shining example of a free society.

Australia in the 1990s seems ready to challenge this notion of itself. In a perfectly understandable urge to acquire a new sense of certainty and security, Australians seem to be developing something of a pro-regulation mentality.

The upheavals of the past 20 years have taken their toll: Australia (like many other societies who are in the process of redefining themselves) is suffering from a virtual epidemic of anxiety, simply because the life of the pioneer is a stressful and unstable life, and anxiety is the outcome of such sustained instability.

But, while the search for new securities and certainties is perfectly understandable, it is leading many Australians to believe that more rules and regulations might provide a welcome sense that "things are back under control".

The desire for simple certainty is showing up in the rise of fundamentalism — in religion, in feminism, in environmentalism and in economic rationalism — but it is also emerging in a disturbing willingness to give up freedoms in favour of tighter controls.

The present mood of the community favours more regulation of *anything* which would appear to introduce a greater sense of stability and control. In this mood, Australians would be likely to favour reregulation of the banking system; more active regulation of advertising; the reintroduction of capital punishment; more stringent controls over the behaviour of company directors; more harsh sentencing procedures ... even when corporations and professional groups begin exploring the need for codes of ethics, the present mood of insecurity tends to encourage the drift into codes of regulation and practice.

Australians are even now wondering whether "we have had too much freedom for our own good", such is their sense of insecurity and their desire to create new rules to live by. Even conscience has become a suitable case for regulation!

Will we, in our desire to deal with the anxiety of the age, give away too many freedoms and submit ourselves to extensive regulations which we will ultimately come to resent? Will Australians become so acquiescent that they will prefer regulation to the exercise of judgement? Is our treatment of smokers, for example, a signpost to an even harsher policy of social engineering? Before we decide whether Australians *really* value their freedoms, we had better wait and see.

A TRADITIONAL WESTMINSTER-STYLE PARLIAMENTARY DEMOCRACY?

One traditional dimension of any analysis of the Australian identity has been our extraordinary stable political system and our uncritical acceptance of the Westminster-style procedures of adversarial, two-party politics.

If we think that that has been a defining characteristic of our identity then, looking to the republican debate, we had better wait and see what the future holds.

In fact, there are two signs which point to a new instability in Australian politics:

- The increasing inability of voters to distinguish between the philosophical positions of the major parties has raised serious questions about the continuing relevance of a two-party system, and has created an explosion in the number of swinging voters (up from 5 percent 20 years ago to 30 percent today).

- Deepening cynicism about the quality of political life, and the appropriateness of our political structures, has led to an urge to debate the system itself.

The republican debate has attracted a great deal of attention in this community, even before Australians were clear about what kind of republic they might be offered. However, my research would suggest that, as the debate matures, it is about much more than the simple question of whether Australia should finally cut its ties with the British Monarchy. Increasingly, Australians are looking for the opportunity to debate almost every aspect of the current political system, and it seems very likely that if they are offered nothing more than the so-called "minimalist" position in a referendum on a republic, they will reject it.

The community has developed a taste for rethinking the system, and they are unlikely to be satisfied by minimalism. If we are to become a republic then we are certainly going to want to play a part in the popular election of a Head of State. But we are also ready to debate the question of whether an adversarial two-party system is the best we can do; whether we need 15 Houses of Parliament for the good government of 17 million people; whether there is something about the political process which kills the idealism of those who enter it; and so on.

Whether it turns out that Australians are interested in a republic or not, my assessment is that they are certainly in favour of a major rethink about our political institutions, structures and processes. If the nature of politics in Australia will be a defining characteristic of our identity, then we had better wait and see what will evolve.

MULTI RACIAL OR MULTICULTURAL?

Australians have traditionally characterised Australian society as being multi racial, and their traditional view has been that migrants should be assimilated. Even today, the typical Australian view of immigration is that migrants are welcome here as long as they are prepared to embrace the Australian way of life and its values, to make the learning of English a top priority, and to leave their own racial and cultural tensions behind. Although Australians have welcomed the enrichment of Australian culture through immigration, they have been very impatient with any sign of immigrants "clinging" to their cultural origins at the expense of the assimilation process.

More recently, of course, Australians have been confronted with the concept of multiculturalism and it is probably fair to suggest that most of them are still puzzled and perplexed by it. They wonder what "multiculturalism" will actually mean for the evolution of an Australian identity, and they fear that it may lead to fragmentation rather than cultural enrichment.

At present, anxiety about the meaning of multiculturalism is often focussed on the growing Asian presence in Australia, although, with only 4 percent of the population having been born in South-East Asia, Australians find the suggestion of Australia being described as "an Asian country" rather silly: they cannot easily accept that Australia is "Asian" except in terms of the geographical accident of its location, and in terms of the emerging realities of our economic links with Asia.

So, as with so many other aspects of the Australian way of life, the only thing to be said about Australians' sense of their cultural identity — as they come to terms with the possible meanings of multiculturalism — is that the situation is unclear ... and we had better wait and see.

Given that Australia is undergoing such a program of social, cultural, economic, political and technological change, it is hardly surprising that the characteristic of contemporary Australian society is its instability, and that the characteristic of Australians is their sense of anxiety and insecurity.

Of course, Australia is not alone in its latest preoccupation with the redefinition of its national identity. Most western societies are experiencing similar socio-economic upheaval and, by comparison with the countries of eastern Europe, Australia is a cultural millpond.

Nevertheless, there are some particular confusions for Australia, if only because we are trying to cope with such radical changes at a time when we have not been at the business of nationhood for very long and when even the concept of Australian citizenship is not yet 50 years old. Culturally speaking, we are a very young society and we are now caught in a somewhat "adolescent" tension between the appeal of a childhood when we were dependent upon Mother England and the appeal of an adulthood in which we take our place in the international community as a nation in our own right. That tension is increased by the apparently conflicting claims of our British heritage, our long exposure to the influence of American culture, and our geopolitical location in Asia. Some identity crisis seems appropriate!

Without wanting to push the analogy too far, it is perhaps to be expected that, at such a tumultuous and unstable time in our sociocultural development, we would be exhibiting some of the classic insecurities associated with adolescence:

- We show signs of dramatic mood swings in everything from our opinions about politicians to our faith in Australia's future.
- We seem genuinely confused about what we really want from our immigrants and, indeed, from foreign investors — fluctuating between gratitude for their assistance and a fiercely independent desire to "keep them in their place".
- We seem to be in the grip of the "have-it-all" mentality: we want to combine low inflation, full employment *and* record foreign debt; we would like to enjoy low taxation *and* generous social security provisions; we would like to restore Australian manufacturing to a healthy state *and* freely exercise our right to purchase imported products . . . our list of incompatible goals is impressive.

The current nostalgia boom may be another symptom of our deep uncertainties about whether we want to cling to the past or grow into a new maturity. The boom in rural nostalgia, in particular, is particularly symbolic: for one of the most urbanised nations on earth, our faith in the idea of "rural virtue" is particularly touching. Growing numbers of Australians harbour the fantasy that, if only they could move to the bush, life would be improved and they would be able to be more closely in touch with "real" Australian values and "real" Australian culture. Indeed, there is a very powerful rural dimension in the sense of national identity for many Australians.

In fact, there is not about to be a mass migration back to the bush: we indulge our country fantasies and our rural nostalgia in less demanding ways. We install country kitchens in our inner-city houses; we wear elastic-sided RM Williams boots; we drive our four-wheel-drive vehicles which never actually leave the bitumen but which stand as a symbol of our *potential* to return to the bush.

All of these symbols are harmless enough . . . yet they are one more sign that we are still in the process of coming to terms with who we really are, and we are still at the stage of denying that we are a heavily urbanised society.

I have suggested that, because Australia is going through such a radical period of redefinition of its cultural institutions and conventions, we are still a very long way from being able to define our national identity. I have suggested that, when it comes to many of the traditional features of our "identity", we shall simply have to wait and see whether they are going to survive the present Age of Redefinition.

But what might be the signs that we are beginning to become comfortable with a new sense of national identity? What will be the signs that our present insecurities and uncertainties are being resolved in favour of a clearer sense of who we are and what we might become?

One of those signs will be when we begin to *celebrate our diversity*, rather than wringing our hands over our differences.

Another will be when we develop a new sense of *shared values* arising from the inescapable sense that we are one society and one culture — a culture with as much diversity as you like, but a deep and underlying sense that we know what kind of society we want to be.

A third sign will be our willingness to accept that we are *all* New Australians; that we are all caught up in the process of creating a new Australia. Our cultural maturity depends upon acknowledging that our identity is changing, and upon having the patience to accept that, given time, our new identity will evolve. Do we have the patience — and the courage — to content ourselves with descriptions of that process, rather than prescriptions for its outcome?

COMMENTARY

AUSTRALIA IS NOT ALONE IN REDEFINING ITS IDENTITY

Alison Broinowski

We are by no means the only country in the process of redefining our identity and to assume that we are is actually slightly adolescent in itself. The Japanese are deeply involved in the redefinition of their nationality. Debate over "true identity" has been going on for a decade. In the United States there has been "The End of History Debate" which is nothing more or less than exactly that. How can one possibly look at what is going on in the European Community and not say that national redefinition is not going on there? In Eastern Europe and a number of other places it is a millennial thing. It is worldwide, and it is not just us.

CAN AUSTRALIA BECOME A REPUBLIC?

Q   (to Thomas Keneally)

Assuming we want Australia to become a republic, which I do not, how could it be accomplished?

Thomas Keneally

It would have to be a question of minimalism. When we talk about a republic, a lot of people say it is an attempt to do away with the States; or it is an attempt to do away with the powers of the Senate. It is not. Those questions are waiting to be dealt with in the next century along with the questions of whether to have guaranteed civil rights in the Constitution, and whether to reflect in the Constitution the way we are actually governed. The Prime Minister and Cabinet, for example, are not mentioned in the Constitution. I think that for the moment, a minimalist republic is all we are going to get. I think that will be enough to produce some resolution. This is such an enormous symbolic and emotional issue, far more symbolic than abandoning, say, appeals to the Privy Council. Because of that, it will be an extensive debate and it will involve the ultimate acquaintance between the Australian people and their own Constitution. Out of that will come the other questions.

We are only minimalist because the Constitution says we have to be. We have to get a majority of people in a majority of States to vote for it. Therefore, what sort of constitution will we have? We will have a republic which is based on our version of the Westminster system, the Australian version. Anything else in the next ten years is probably not desirable in my opinion. Australians, by becoming a republic, will get control of their own Constitution and will adjust it in the next century.

RECONCILIATION WITH ABORIGINALS

Q (to Hugh Mackay)

In relation to the recent extraordinarily ill-informed debate that has been taking place in Australia on the *Mabo* decision, will this decision increase or decrease the likelihood of developing a treaty with the Aboriginal people? Would that be a sign of us finally growing up, getting to the point where we do actually sign a treaty and put down some kind of symbol of good faith, even if it goes no further than that? Has any research been done on what people understand generally about the *Mabo* decision, and what kind of reaction has there been?

Hugh Mackay

We have certainly been getting some research feedback on *Mabo* from the community. The community is totally confused by what the *Mabo* decision implies, what the subsequent debate is all about, and the great uneasiness in the community about *Mabo* is a symptom of an even deeper uneasiness about the larger Aboriginal question. This is a community in which white Australians have not got the slightest idea what black Australians actually want. Neither do they know how what they want could be incorporated into Australian society, or into the sense of an Australian identity. Just as when people watch news of Bosnia on their television, all they can say about it is, "this is why we are uneasy about immigration — we don't want all those tensions being brought in here — we have not got the foggiest idea who the good guys and bad guys are — it is very hard to watch a war without taking sides, so we are confused by that". In the same way that Bosnia triggers all that uneasiness about other peoples' problems coming here, so *Mabo* triggers all that uneasiness about what we have never really come to terms with — what the relationship between black and white Australians should be. My suspicion is that the *Mabo* debate is actually hardening attitudes against Aborigines. There has been so much uneasiness and so much contradictory information, that people are taking refuge in the most appalling prejudice. There is a much harder edge to the way people talk about concepts of reconciliation.

MULTICULTURALISM

Q

I used to work in multicultural affairs. I have been a migrant to this country. What is multiculturalism? When I worked in multicultural affairs and visited different ethnic communities, I was astounded about differences and how little we all knew about each other. Are we not all very confused?

Hugh Mackay

That echoes very much what my own reading of the community is. The peculiarity of the Australian multicultural experiment is one of the reasons why our situation in terms of redefining our identity is a bit different from some other countries. Many Australians are still very uncomfortable with the word "multiculturalism".

Q

I am a New Australian. I believe that Australia is a white European culture, and no matter how much we convince ourselves we are culturally diverse or a multicultural society, the rest of the world still thinks of us as a white culture. In dealing with our national identity, do we need to change this image?

Thomas Keneally

It is very interesting that Australians are not perceived as being anything more than British. I noticed that Americans (I have worked at the University of California) are astounded to hear that there are Yugoslavs and Greeks here. They are astounded to hear that Melbourne is such a big Greek city and they are then astounded to hear that there are Asians here. They still perceive us as a place where women are in the same position as blacks are in South Africa. Australian women are often commiserated with while they are there! They believe too that we are not ethnically diverse. On the other hand, the great triumph of our immigration program is that racism is largely only verbal in Australia, except against Aboriginals. That triumph is obscured internationally, because we do not project a real picture of who we are, and again, one of the problems with that is the monarchy.

Hugh Mackay

There is no doubt that we are seen internationally as much more of a white European culture than we actually are. We have been here, in terms of European civilisation, loosely defined, for 200 years, and for 175 of those years, effectively we were a "White Australia". The White Australia Policy was only dismantled 25 years ago, and so the attitudes of other cultures towards this culture change as slowly as human attitudes generally do change, at a glacial pace. We have a very significant marketing job on our hands to convince other people, especially our Asian neighbours, that the White Australia Policy is a thing of the past. We have to remind ourselves and acknowledge that it is a thing of the very recent past.

II

VOICES FROM MULTICULTURAL AUSTRALIA

INTRODUCTION

Jeanette Beaumont

To articulate a concept of a cultural identity which has meaning for Australian nationhood in the 1990s is no simple task. Thomas Keneally argues in Chapter 1 of this book that there is an evolving national identity significantly different from 19th century nationalism. And Hugh Mackay has pointed to the myths and to some of the realities.

Should we seek after or encourage a sense of national identity? What value is there in the pursuit of definition? Can it lead to repression, conformism and exclusion? In Part II, cultural identity is discussed on a more personal level by five men and women of diverse backgrounds. In different ways they are representative of Australian society and its many cultures.

Andrew Riemer's contribution is as a writer and academic who also regularly reviews books for the *Sydney Morning Herald*. He has written a prize-winning account of his own experience of life between two worlds, the old order in Europe and the new in Australia, *Inside Outside Life: Between Two Worlds*[1] was published in 1992. The *Habsburg Café*[2] was published in 1993. He came to Sydney from Budapest in 1946 as a ten-year-old who could not speak English.

Jillian Oppenheimer is fifth-generation Australian. Her Anglo-Scottish ancestors began grazing sheep in the New England district of New South Wales in the 1840s. She sees herself as a representative of rural Australia. She is interested in history, heritage and conservation, and is deputy president of the National Trust in New South Wales. With her husband, Bruce Mitchell, she has written a book entitled *An Australian Clan, The Nivisons of New England*,[3] about her family, its old homestead and property.

Devleena Ghosh was born and educated in India and holds an MA degree in Comparative Literature from Jadavpur University, Calcutta. She was an activist in the women's and literacy movements in India and is interested in women's studies and popular culture. She has published numerous translations from Hindi, French and

English into Bengali, and is currently a lecturer in Hindi at the University of Sydney. She is married to John Berwick.

John Berwick was born in Sydney, where his father's family had reunited after his father had been sent to an Aboriginal mission at Cowra. John is a distinguished historian with a doctorate in Indian history. In 1991 he was the Pacific correspondent for the *Calcutta Telegraph*. His special interest is the role of education in social change, and law in South-East Asia. He is a practising barrister of the Supreme Court of NSW.

Sakuko Matsui came to Australia from Japan in 1961. She is associate professor of Japanese at the University of Sydney, and was the first Japanese-born lecturer appointed to an Australian university after World War II. Her special interest is Japanese literature.

ALLEGIANCE TO A COMMUNITY: ALLEGIANCE TO A COUNTRY

Jillian Oppenheimer

I am descended from people who were something like *The Man from Snowy River*. They were shearing the rams in the days when Tom Roberts was painting them. They are also part of the imagery of Russell Drysdale. Even the mythology of *Crocodile Dundee* had roots in their being. But that mystique has deteriorated somewhat into a category of yobbos and ockers!

The people of the bush were part of Australia's backbone and I think the things they stood for in the past could be looked to in the future. But if the cities continue to look towards the coast and not towards the living inner heart, the "bushies" could become the peasants of the future. We are training for that very well at present with the drought and the economic recession!

Of my 16 great great grandparents, 12 came from Scotland, 2 from the Channel Islands and 2 from England. (Unfortunately I have not got a convict amongst them.) I have always considered myself a Scottish Australian. I have no difficulty at all about feeling that I have a dual identity. I empathise with more recent newcomers, from Greece, Italy, India or wherever, who obviously have allegiance to the home of their birth and have become Australians. I think that you can have a dual nationality, if only in your own soul. I have a strong allegiance primarily to Australia, but when I think of Australia, much as I like to dip into the city for a splash of culture with concerts and art galleries, I never feel spiritually at home until I get back to the gum trees and the bush.

There are two aspects to identity. One is allegiance to a group, to a community, and in the outback particularly to small rural communities. Beyond that is allegiance to a country.

Families on the land for 150 years or more feel a strong commitment and loyalty to the particular area in which they have lived for a long period of time. I am fortunate enough to live in the house that was built by my great grandfather, and when I think of Australia when I am overseas, that is where my thoughts go. They do not go to Sydney, they do not go to the beaches and the areas where the majority of the Australian population lives. I always feel most comfortable, most at ease when there is no feeling of claustrophobia, where there is space and a very clear, brilliant, unpolluted sky with wonderful clouds and star effects at night. The land, to me personally, is enormously important, and for that reason, I also feel strongly for the Aboriginal people who were displaced by my forebears, and to whom we have a strong commitment to do something, in the future, in order to make sure that they can be part of a community of Australians. To be an Australian is to have a sense of fair play, and a sense of egalitarianism. I think that there is a healthy attitude of cutting down tall poppies, not tolerating people who consider themselves superior or arrogant, a feeling of pragmatism ("she'll be right, mate"), and a concern for our fellow human beings. These attitudes are still strong in the community, particularly in the bush, and are still genuinely Australian.

JAPAN OR AUSTRALIA? CHOOSING WHERE TO LIVE

Sakuko Matsui

Australian individualism contrasts strangely to Japanese conformity. Students develop individualism in Australia while at university and the system allows it. The system was what I liked when I first came here. The system encourages the students to be individuals to have individual interests, while in Japan individualism is difficult.

I came to Australia in 1961, by what was called "One Class Cargo Passenger". It took me 11 days straight from Kobe to Sydney. I asked the captain what the ship was carrying. The reply was coal and wool from Australia, but nothing from Japan! That was in 1961. Soon after, we started seeing Japanese cameras, radios and then cars. When I first came here, I came straight to the Women's College at Sydney University. The people I met were so open minded. Although I had majored in English from a university in Japan, I had studied mostly reading, and while I could read Shakespeare, I could hardly speak English! I found the Australian language students much more sophisticated than their Japanese counterparts. I find them so even now. When I started teaching Japanese at the University of Sydney we had about 25 students. Now we have more than 500 undergraduates, plus post-graduates. I have always found Australian students relatively (compared with Japanese) hard working. I often wonder why they are studying Japanese. It is such a difficult language. They seem to do it because they are interested. And this is in stark contrast to Japanese universities where, even now, students study because they have got to get a degree, or they go into a university, into a particular course or department, because their high school teacher thinks that is an appropriate place, judging from their marks and nothing else.

As to my still keeping Japanese nationality, it is just a matter of convenience. If I lose my Japanese nationality, it would be very awkward. I would hate to be fingerprinted as an alien when I go back to Japan! Then I could not stay longer than my tourist visa would allow and all my family is there. In Australia, I have never had trouble as a permanent resident. Of course I cannot vote, but I do not miss that very much. I never missed it in Japan either. It has never occurred to me to really take up Australian citizenship, perhaps I am apolitical. Japan is a less free, less individualistic country. The Australian bureaucracy has never troubled me about being a permanent resident here.

There are now about 500 Japanese migrating to Australia every year. That number has increased in recent years, but until last year there were probably about 2000 in Sydney and 6000 all over Australia. The majority of the 500 who come to Australia each year come here just to see what it is like. Japanese in recent years have tended to look more positively at what used to be considered as the "uncouthness" or "unculturedness" of Australians. In their view the Australian people are perhaps more friendly than polite, but they are frank. Of course I have heard some Japanese businessmen, particularly in Sydney, say "there's no culture here", and I think that is nonsense.

What interests me about Australian culture is that the University of Sydney has one of the oldest Departments of Oriental Studies in the world — it was set up in 1918. It is interesting that Sydney University started with Japanese language and culture rather than Chinese. The university has produced half-a-dozen academics who either hold chairs of Japanese in Australia or are heads of departments in universities in Australia, in New Zealand, or in Europe.

THE LOSSES AND GAINS OF LIVING IN ANOTHER COUNTRY

Devleena Ghosh

When I came to Australia in 1981, it was really a very different country. I was brought up in an internationalist household. My father was a left-wing internationalist and we were always told we were citizens of the world. When I came to Australia, I found in fact I was not. I remember being in floods of tears because I had only seen two people on the street all day, or because the shops all shut at 5.00 pm!

My view about being a migrant is that you lose a lot, and one of the main things you lose is language. I was fortunate in being able to speak English fairly well when I came here, but even so, on going into a pub in Australia and being told it was my "shout", I thought it was a quaint initiation custom that Australians had of getting up on the table and screaming loudly, and I had to be told it actually meant to go up to the bar and buy drinks for everyone. Those little things are perhaps not distressing, but they continue to remind you that you are really somewhat different, and that you really are not part of the mass community. I think language is important — I am very conscious when I go back to India that my Bengali, which is my first language, suffers because I have been speaking English for so long.

What has been gained? India is a very patriarchal culture and being a woman in India is difficult — especially to be a woman who attempts to be liberated and emancipated. The sense in Australia of space, and I do not mean just physical space but personal space, was absolutely liberating for me — to be able to walk out on the street, to wear the clothes I liked, to smoke a cigarette if I wanted to... In India, when you get onto a train you are asked your name, your father's name, your job, your salary, your father's salary, your husband, do you have children, why not... The sense of actually being able to be yourself and not answerable to those around was a new freedom.

India is a fascinating society which I really love, but I enjoy being able to detach myself. This has given me a perspective on India which is important to me. That is one of the things I have gained.

Another problem with being a migrant in this country is that you do live a variety of roles. You live a role as a black woman, you live a role as a person who speaks a different language, you live a role as a migrant, you also live as an Indian within yourself. Where I think the real problems of national identity lie, and why I am so ambivalent about it, is that to find something that actually includes these roles, but does not disrupt any one of them, is exceptionally difficult.

What is happening in India now is that Muslims in that country are being asked to identify themselves as Hindu Muslims. That is ridiculous. It is a contradiction in terms. The attempt at a homogeneous identity is dangerous. We should approach such definitions with great caution.

When I think about national identity, I go back to my childhood, and remember my father saying to me, "You are not just an Indian. You are a citizen of the world". It is a very simplistic thing to say, extremely simplistic. Like all simple things, like all clichés, it only has a degree of truth in it.

It is disturbing for a person like me who comes from a very old culture to come to a country where the original "old culture" of the Aboriginal people — an oral culture of however many thousand years — is so invisible. What I saw when I first came was a European culture. The sense of confronting what is a dominant culture which has in fact pushed the original culture out is, for people like me, an interesting anomaly. This must contribute a great deal to the question of Australia's culture and identity.

I feel much more strongly Indian in Australia than I do in India. This is a funny thing. Here I identify myself as an Indian, when I go back to India, I am constantly saying, "this is a terrible place, in Australia I did not have to put up with this". Perhaps this is a normal reaction. Although I do identify myself as an Indian and there is a chance in the next ten years or so that I might go back to India permanently, I think what I have gained over here is a sense of an extra commitment and an extra responsibility, rather than having lost those things. When I go back to India, the foreign country I am most interested in is Australia. I have lived here and I have been happy here.

THE NATIONAL DEBATE THREATENS SOCIAL STRUCTURES

John Berwick

I am not particularly enthusiastic about promulgating the concept of national identity, but that does not mean that I am not interested in Australia. And I would certainly hope that does not mean that I am not appropriately grateful for the opportunities in terms of education and other facilities that Australia has given to people of my generation in the late 1960s by our parents, who had built on foundations laid in the Depression and later.

However, it seems to me that a deep scepticism is appropriate. I am particularly sceptical about the current structure of the republican debate. I certainly do not make these remarks as a monarchist, I speak from the left. As constitutional structures around the world collapse in a welter of tribalism, with all that implies, we ought to be extremely wary of a debate about national identity that both includes and excludes. I think there is a lot of dragooning going on. I feel deeply that the structure of the debate as it has occurred so far has more to do with making Australia a suitable productive unit for interaction with nations in South-East Asia, who have had traditionally dissident structures such as trade unions all but destroyed. A substantial component of the direction which republicanism is taking is the dismantling of many of the older dissident structures, which the group of people in Australian society from which I come — what used to be called the "working class" — were able to utilise in order to integrate themselves with the wider polity. What I am concerned about is that any debate about national identity which is driven largely if not entirely by the need to make Australia a more productive Asian-type economic unit, has a long-range danger of excluding the traditional working-class sections of this society. It is becoming clear as history unfolds that many of the older structures of national integration, particularly trade unions, had connections with older tory traditions (19th century British tory with a small "t", for want of a better term, not the Tory Party as such) that were not particularly obvious at the time when those institutions had their greatest influence on Australian life. As various historical imperatives unfold and institutions become weaker in national eyes, their older tory connections are becoming clearer.

It is assumed that the people likely to be excluded from any concept of our national identity are Asians. My view is somewhat different. Living where I do in Marrickville, one of the most multicultural areas in Australia, and one which has a high Asian component, I can see that Asians will eventually draw on their traditions of close relationships within the extended family, on their capacity to accumulate capital through family and social relationships, and this will enable them to integrate themselves into the type of productive future that leaders of all of our parties seem to be putting forward as the only goal for Australia to satisfactorily pursue. Asians will not be "out", they will be "in" in a big way — maybe not in this generation but within a very small number of generations. The people who will be out will be large sections of the traditional working class who have been forced out of their traditional inner-city domain, which had an important historical role of integrating them with a wider metropolitan culture. The old cultures of Woolloomooloo-Darlinghurst-Paddington and so on, with which I was familiar in my childhood through my parents, through my father in particular, are now being forced out onto the edges of our cities. These people are being denied resources, and in fact are in danger of dropping into an historical black hole and failing to find a satisfactory place in the productive unit that Australia is very likely to become. And what that leads to historically, I fear, is the very real danger of the emergence of (once again, to use all these old-fashioned historical terms) a proletariat which will be very much outside anything that could be satisfactorily described as having a national identity.

Futhermore, something has to be said about the Aboriginal perspective. My father, when he first came to live in Paddington, actually came from the Eurambie Aboriginal Mission at Cowra. His experience was a typical one of the time in that he was the youngest of a family of six, and when the parents, for various reasons, had separated, the children were split up as per the welfare policy of the day and individually sent around to work on farms. Then my eldest aunt gathered them up, determined this was not going to happen to her family. She took them from the countryside and melded them into the suburb of Paddington. Insofar as I have any claim to speak on behalf of Aboriginal people, that is it, as tenuous as it may be. I have always been acutely aware of that historical experience. If one is ever silly enough to raise that part of one's experience, the first reaction is always (and this comes from blacks and whites, perhaps more intensely from blacks) "that's all very well, but do you identify as an Aboriginal?". The simple answer is that I identify as a person of Aboriginal descent. It is a shame in terms of the possibility of a national identity and the debate about Aboriginal experiences, that a broader classification does not have more validity on both sides of the great divide that seems to have emerged after *Mabo*.

As to the historical nexus between Aboriginal identity and the national identity of Australia, it has always seemed to me that the beginnings of Australia's debate about its international role occurred in the late 1960s and early 1970s. There was the Vietnam War, an experience that my generation can remember quite strongly, but at the same time in 1971, there was the Springbok football tour. I attended a student debate at that time on whether Australia was inadequately facing up to its international responsibilities. There were present some young Aboriginal activists, Paul Coe was one, and a number of others who have now become quite well known in Aboriginal affairs, who expressed the view "this is all very well, but it is entirely inadequate — a new era of land rights struggle on behalf of the Aboriginal people must now begin". The challenge was to integrate the two political activities, the two political trends that had emerged in and around the opposition to the Springbok tour. Here was the genesis of what I call the modern land rights movement. I am quite well aware that in the 1920s and 1930s there were other traditions — sometimes specifically political and usually left wing. And of course there were the movements of stockmen in the Northern Territory in the 1960s. But in the 1970s there was an interesting return to the great domestic issue in Australian history.

To turn again to Australia's relations with Asia, what is almost never discussed in the debate is the role of India and what India might or might not contribute. For the nations that are immediately around us, particularly places such as Thailand and Indonesia, over the last couple of millennia the dominant cultural force has been the civilisational ideas that have originated in the Indian subcontinent. I certainly would not claim they have been purely Hindu ideals — that is a total misnomer — but there are ideas that have originated in India, that have their origin in basic concepts of Indian philosophy, particularly in Buddhist conceptions, and often agnostic conceptions of what humanity might be about. It does seem to be the case, sadly, that the great civilisation that has existed in the Indian subcontinent for some millennia is now in a state of crisis and has lost a great deal of its historical direction. India's secular, classically 19th-century constitution, which has governed it since independence, does not seem to be providing an appropriate inspiration for the people, almost a billion of whom have lived under its umbrella for the past 50-odd years.

Constitutional changes are an historical development which is fraught with danger for Australia and for countries in the whole South-East Asian region. In our attempt to immediately link up with the productive potential of China and other nations with which we seem to be currently obsessed, the changes that are occurring are affecting the core of our cultures, at the deepest levels, the things which have been a source of ideas and inspiration. These are difficult issues that Australia will have to confront. There does not seem a great deal of debate about these ideas in our enthusiasm for economic solutions.

AN ORGANIC AND DIVERSE NATIONAL IDENTITY

Andrew Riemer

I should not tangle with the question of national identity, because it is something about which I feel profoundly ambivalent and a little alarmed. When I came to this country in 1947, at the age of 10, the phrase "New Australian" (which Hugh Mackay mentions on p 13) had not yet been invented. Anybody who was not Australian (and everybody knew then what an Australian was) was a "wog", a "reffo" or a "DP" (displaced person). I was one of those wogs, reffos or DPs who came here in 1947. The country I had come from, one of those troubled central European countries, Hungary, is again bitterly trying to sort out its national identity after 40-45 years of communism. That country had, in the course of my early childhood, engaged in a very strenuous attempt to establish its own national identity. By so doing, it decided to exclude people. Some of those people were families such as my family, and thousands if not millions of others who had lived in that country and been citizens for several generations. I am, therefore, ambivalent, concerned and worried about any society's attempts to define its national characteristics and its national identity, even perhaps its national goals and national aims. I sometimes wonder whether it would not be best merely to let it evolve, however it will.

Nevertheless in the case of national identities and national prototypes, perhaps even national fictions, there are profound myths, legends and beliefs that become part and parcel of the cultural fabric of a society. It is those things that we ought to try to explore. There is something in Jillian Oppenheimer's interests — the importance of the land and of rural Australia — which pervades the myths, legends and prototypes of the Australian national identity. I wonder whether the sense of fair play and egalitarianism that she refers to is not also similar to the powerful national myths or legends that societies carry around with them. European migrants of my parents' generation brought to the Australian culture and the Australian national identity a rather embarrassing contempt for non-European cultures. The endless lamentation about being obliged to live in this cultural desert amongst these uncivilised people is a tricky topic.

I am very conscious that these ideas are equally applicable to that rather macho Hungarian society that bred me, and which is again attempting to rediscover its national identity in a fairly sexist and racist fashion. The resurgence of the new European nations to the East of what used to be the Iron Curtain is worrying. On the other hand, the notion that our existing national identity can encompass a very large number of things is what saves the current debate in Australia from devolving into nationalistic strutting.

A society is something fluid, constantly changing, being redefined perhaps almost as soon as it has defined itself. What is significant about the contributors to this chapter is that only two of the five would have been classified as Australian in 1947. When I stepped off that ship at Woolloomooloo with my parents, I realised that whatever we were we were not, or were not yet, Australians.

On Devleena Ghosh's point about the loss and gain of the migrant experience, even after spending almost 50 years in this country, I am conscious of the fact that I have gained a great deal and I have also lost a little bit. I think that little bit of loss is probably well worth losing. Nevertheless, inevitably for people like us there is a sense of the provisional in a commitment one makes to a country or a society. The possibility always existed that things might have been otherwise.

Jillian Oppenheimer and John Berwick were born in this country and have the type of connection with Australia which I, despite having spent the greater part of my life here, cannot yet fully experience. It would be foolish to pretend that anyone who was not born in the country can fully experience that commitment or that togetherness with a land and its implications. I am very conscious of the perspective that Sakuko Matsui brings to this discussion, her sense of remaining a Japanese citizen as a matter of convenience, of being a part of this society and yet not making an absolute commitment to this society. This is something that I share, because I think it is difficult to make an absolute commitment to a society unless you are born into it, and unless you have some sort of mythological or even perhaps religious roots within it.

A person of Sakuko's eminence, who has made such a valued contribution to the intellectual life of an Australian university and of the community, who has influenced the lives of so many young people over a number of years, surely has the right to consider herself as an Australian, despite her Japanese nationality. Devleena Ghosh, who is the most recent of us to come to this country, has also made a contribution in the years that she has been here. Is that not sufficient for her to consider herself as an Australian? Could we perhaps not consider ourselves as being Australians for some years, in my case Hungarian for some years, and whatever else ten years down the track?

Role playing — what I think of sometimes as mimicry — is vitally important, not only to the migrant experience, but in the attempt to understand national identities, national characteristics. Devleena claims that she feels less Indian now when she goes to India. I feel very Australian when I go to Hungary. Some sort of cultural possibility emerges out of the melding or the meshing of different types of national or cultural identity.

COMMENTARY

RELATIONS BETWEEN RURAL AUSTRALIA AND THE CITIES

Q

Over the years it has been considered that there has been a feeling of uncertainty between the people on the coastline, urban dwellers, and those in the country. People in the cities do not understand the people in the country and their rural problems. As a result of the drought and other difficulties, the population as we know in the country is declining. What is the view of the people living in our rural areas towards the increasing number of migrants who are coming to Australia and who are naturally going to our cities? How are we going to overcome that split in understanding between the city and the country dweller?

Jillian Oppenheimer

This is a real dilemma. Increasingly, the rural population is the remnant of the 19th century British migration wave. This, I think, is unfortunate. I know that there have been efforts through the years by service groups to bring Vietnamese and other refugees to rural areas and they have come, stayed for a short time and drifted back, understandably perhaps, to their own community groups in the suburbs of the metropolitan cities. It is quite apparent that the changing face of the population in Sydney is more Asian, more multicultural, and I welcome that. We are moving on and our population is changing and flexible. The sense of history of the earlier migrants is being diluted in urban areas, whereas it remains more static and conservative in the country. The population in the country is diminishing. They are under stress. Certainly there is stress in the city but of a different kind. There is an increasing danger of a widening gulf of "us" and "them". There has always been a "city and the bush" conflict — and it is not lessening. I fear it will increase and I urge people to look towards the countryside and try to understand the problems there, as I always urge upon country people to look to the cities and understand the modern and increasingly stressful situation which is occurring because of crowding and other 20th century problems.

HEALTH PROBLEMS AND SOCIAL PROBLEMS CAUSED BY MARGINALISATION

Marie Bashir

I share Dr Berwick's great concern with the marginalisation of some groups in our society, particularly what would formerly have been called the "old Australian working class". And I also share Jillian Oppenheimer's unbounded optimism for the future success of multiculturalism amongst our migrant groups. I wonder how the twain can be made to meet? Already the health problems and the social problems amongst the marginalised groups are serious, particularly amongst the younger members.

John Berwick

The only way health problems and social problems can be addressed is by a resurgence of the role of the state in modern life. That goes against all current wisdom as to what needs to be done in terms of the economic and social difficulties that we find ourselves in. My own historical experience is that education and expanded educational facilities give both hope and opportunity and are symbolic of a society's commitment to all sections that make up the society. And this is simply my own life experience. I had the opportunity to go to university in the late 1960s, and no one from my family had gone much beyond primary school. The deteriorating educational facilities that are offered to younger people in the far western suburbs of Sydney is symbolic of society at large. A lack of national will and a failure of traditional political institutions to find the resources to integrate those people into society, in the way people of my generation were, will have dire implications for this society. There are other factors of course.

UNION MOVEMENT IN AUSTRALIA

Q   (to John Berwick)

I do not feel the addition of other nationalities into Australia can mean anything but good. What I think Australia suffers from today, is a divisive situation of a different sort. Is a union movement that is divisive not bad for Australia?

John Berwick

In spite of the fact that it seemed in the 1940s and 1950s that trade unions were at odds with at least some sections of society, with hindsight it is clear to me that in fact they were one of the major integrating forces in this society. It is lamentable that the concept of their being such a force should drop out of the national consciousness. The idea that trade unions were purely responsible for corporatism — the dragooning of large numbers of working-class people into productive structures that are appropriate for contemporary capitalism, is a limitation to their historical role and a loss of their historical significance.

IS AUSTRALIA IMPROVING SOCIALLY AND ECONOMICALLY?

Q

When Andrew Riemer and Sakuko Matsui arrived in Australia, it was probably one of the top four countries in the world in terms of standard of living. Now we are probably about twentieth. In terms of Australia's national identity, have we lost the individualism that perhaps we might have had 30 years ago that made Australia a more successful country economically and socially than it is now?

Andrew Riemer

I am again worried about definitions. Was the Australia I came to a better place than it is now? In some respects it obviously was. I think it was probably easier for people to make a living. It was probably easier for people to enjoy the benefits of a bountiful land and the sunshine. But in some respects, it seems to me that the Australia of 1993, even in the cities, is a much better place than the Australia of 1947 and 1950, and perhaps a small amount of that is a result not only of racial mixing, but cultural mixing and mixing of attitudes, mixing of philosophies, mixing of religions, which have made Sydney into the melting pot that it is. It is one of the things that makes Sydney a very exciting, although at times somewhat disturbing, city. I do think that we are living on the edge of some sort of change, some sort of development. Perhaps culturally, we just ought to let it happen. Our national identity, whatever it is going to be, ought just to emerge.

III

THE CONSTITUTION

INTRODUCTION

Margaret Beazley

Writing in 1993, it is extraordinary to think that the document which has governed Australia for the past 90 years, and which has fashioned the legal, economic and social fabric of our society is an Act proclaimed by a foreign country — for the legislation which we call the Australian Constitution was, in fact, passed as an Act of the British Parliament.[1] To say this of course is to put the matter too simply for, as the next chapters show, the Constitution is very much a document of Australian origin.

The Constitution has proved far from a document of perfection, and increasingly inadequate in a changing world. Its tensions largely arise out of its structure whereby limited powers are vested in the Federal Parliament, with all other governmental powers remaining with the States. And even in the interpretation of the Federal powers there is tension between the federalist or centralist view and the States' rightist view. These structures and tensions are examined in the following chapters. But whatever be the imperfections, it seems almost certain that the Australian Constitution as we know it will remain the basis for whatever form of democracy Australia chooses to adopt in the next century.

This is the premise to which Sir Maurice Byers and Sir Harry Gibbs have written. Sir Maurice, in What the Constitution Says, summarises the main provisions of the Constitution so that readers debating reform have a clear idea of what the present situation is.

In Is Change Recommended? Sir Maurice and Sir Harry cover some of the main issues of constitutional reform. Should the States have responsibility for raising the money they spend? Would a Bill of Rights safeguard human rights in Australia? Do we need a Governor-General?

These chapters are necessarily detailed as the Constitution is a legal document as much as a political one. It deals with the minutiae of power sharing between government and government, and between government and people, and so reforming it involves changing the minutiae. Nevertheless, as Sir Maurice points out, the Constitution is "the birth certificate" of the Australian nation and within its detail is the grand vision of Australian democracy.

Origins of the Australian Constitution

Margaret Beazley

The terms of the Constitution were the product of a constitutional convention which first met in Adelaide in 1897.

That was not the first constitutional convention to be held, however. In 1891, an Australasian convention had been held consisting of representatives of the six Australian colonies and also New Zealand. That convention, the major impetus for which had come from Sir Henry Parkes, the then Premier of New South Wales, drafted a Constitution which contained the framework of the present Constitution. However, the 1891 convention and its resultant document did not proceed, fading with the waning political fortunes of its main protagonist. It was not long before fresh moves were made towards Federation. In 1893, a motion was passed by the Australian Natives Association of Corowa for the election of delegates to a new convention, and this was supported by the 1895 Premiers' conference.

The second convention's draft Constitution was submitted to referenda in four colonies, New South Wales, Victoria, South Australia and Tasmania. Queensland had not been represented at the convention, and Western Australia did not submit the draft to a referendum. Although the referenda succeeded in three States, which was sufficient to refer it to the Imperial Parliament for approval, it was not passed by New South Wales. With some amendments, and a second round of referenda, and with Queensland by this time also approving the draft, the matter was ready to submit to London. Western Australia, however, retained its exclusionary stance and did not submit the draft bill to a referendum until after the Constitution Act had been passed by the British Parliament. However, it did so prior to the commencement of the Commonwealth. Provision had also been made for New Zealand to be in the new federation, but it chose not to do so. The Queen's proclamation pursuant to s 3 of the Constitution Act was issued on 17 September 1900, proclaiming the coming into existence of the Commonwealth of Australia on 1 January 1901.

Sections 3 and 6 of the Constitution Act record this historical context in which Australia became a Federation. They provide:

> 3. **Proclamation of Commonwealth.** — It shall be lawful for the Queen, with the advice of the Privy Council, to declare by proclamation that, on and after a day therein appointed, not being later than one year after the passing of this Act, the people of New South Wales, Victoria, South Australia, Queensland and Tasmania, and also, if Her Majesty is satisfied that the people of Western Australia have agreed thereto, of Western Australia, shall be united in a Federal Commonwealth under the name of the Commonwealth of Australia. But the Queen may, at any time after the proclamation, appoint a Governor-General for the Commonwealth.
>
> 6. **Definitions.** — "The Commonwealth" shall mean the Commonwealth of Australia as established under this Act.
>
> "The States" shall mean such of the colonies of New South Wales, New Zealand, Queensland, Tasmania, Victoria, Western Australia, and South Australia, including the northern territory of South Australia, as for the time being are parts of the Commonwealth, and such colonies or territories as may be admitted into or established by the Commonwealth as States; and each of such parts of the Commonwealth shall be called "a State".
>
> "Original States" shall mean such States as are parts of the Commonwealth as its establishment.

It should not be thought, however, that the draft Constitution was wholeheartedly and uncritically embraced by the Imperial Parliament. A major point of contention was the extent of appeals to the Privy Council. The strength of the second convention's view of independence from Imperial control was reflected in this debate. The draft provided only for appeals in respect of matters involving the public interest affecting another part of Her Majesty's Dominions.

Eventually agreement was reached on the provision which became s 74, which preserved to the High Court the determination of constitutional issues, unless the High Court considered such constitutional issue should be determined by the Privy Council. However, provision was made for appeals by leave to Her Majesty in Council on all other matters. In addition, s 74 permitted the Australian Parliament to enact laws further limiting the right of such appeal. The effect of s 74 was described by Dixon J in *Nelungaloo Pty Ltd v Commonwealth*:[1]

> The fact is that the basic purpose of s 74 and of the principles upon which this court has proceeded has been to confine the final decision of the characteristically federal questions described by s 74 to a jurisdiction exercised within the federal system by a court to which the problems and special conceptions of federalism must become very familiar, not without the hope, perhaps, that thus a body of constitutional doctrine might be developed.

The Commonwealth Parliament did enact legislation to restrict the matters in respect of which appeals could be made to the Privy Council and in 1986, appeals to the Privy Council were abolished altogether by the enactment by the British Parliament, at the request of the Australian Parliament, of the *Australia Act* 1986 (UK). Of equal constitutional although less practical importance was that the *Australia Act* terminated the power of the British Parliament to legislate for the Australian States.

What the Constitution Says

Sir Maurice Byers

The Constitution is the instrument which contains the terms of the union of the Australian people: it established this nation. The form the nation took was that of an "indissoluble Federal Commonwealth under the Crown of the United Kingdom of Great Britain and Ireland and under the Constitution". The terms of the Union had been agreed by the votes of the peoples of all the States. Since the passing of the *Australia Act* 1986, which abolished the power of the Parliament of the United Kingdom to legislate for this country (even if then it could be said still to exist), the Constitution derives its force and efficacy from the will of the people not only in fact but also in law.

An eminent justice of the High Court described the Constitution in these terms:

> The Constitution is not merely an instrument of government of a federation. It is that; but it is more. It is the birth certificate of a nation. It embodies in legal form the sentiment of a people behind the idea of "a nation for a continent and a continent for a nation". On the enactment of the Constitution by the Imperial Parliament the Australian colonies became a Dominion under the Crown, Australia, now in its own right a nation among the nations. Australians became one people. These are things to be remembered because in interpreting the Constitution we are not required to ignore the purpose manifestly behind particular provisions. The Constitution is obviously designed to ensure the powers and position of the States as political elements of a federation. It is equally designed to ensure the power and position and to promote the unity of the new nation called into being.[1]

WHAT THE CONSTITUTION SAYS

Prior to 1 January 1901, what became the various States of the Commonwealth were British colonies inhabiting their present territorial boundaries. For many years prior to 1900 there had been discussions between representatives of the colonies on the desirability of a federal union. Eventually in 1900, the people of the colonies of New South Wales, Victoria, South Australia, Queensland and Tasmania had agreed to the terms they desired and their representatives went to London to ensure that what they had agreed would be passed as an Act of the United Kingdom Parliament. This was then the only legal means by which a binding Act of Federation could be achieved. They were successful in the main. By 17 September 1900 the people of Western Australia had joined them and on that day a proclamation was made pursuant to the *Commonwealth of Australia Constitution Act* declaring "that on and after the First day of January One thousand nine hundred and one the people of New South Wales, Victoria, South Australia, Queensland, Tasmania and Western Australia shall be united in a Federal Commonwealth under the name of the Commonwealth of Australia". Section 9 of the *Commonwealth of Australia Constitution Act* provides:

> The Constitution of the Commonwealth shall be as follows:-
> There follow a heading and what are now the one hundred and twenty nine sections of the Constitution concluding with s 128 which contains the power to alter the terms of the Constitution (s 105A was added by the *Constitution Alteration State Debts Act* 1928).

Thus in form the Constitution consists of what is set out in s 9 of the *Commonwealth of Australia Constitution Act* with which one needs to read what is contained in the Preamble to the Act (from which I have taken the reference to the indissoluble Federal Commonwealth) and ss 2, 3, 5 and 6. Section 2 provides that references in the Act to the Queen extend to Her Majesty's heirs and successors in the sovereignty of the United Kingdom. Section 3 authorises the proclamation establishing the Commonwealth to which proclamation I have already referred; s 5 provides that the Acts of the Commonwealth Parliament are binding on the courts, judges and people of every State and of every part of the Commonwealth notwithstanding anything in the laws of any State and the laws of the Commonwealth shall be in force on all British ships, the Queen's ships of war excepted whose first port of clearance and whose port of destination are in the Commonwealth; and s 6 contains definitions of the Commonwealth, the States and "Original States". Section 5 may be considered now to have been superseded by s 109 of the Constitution, and Commonwealth laws now derive their binding force from the existence of the Commonwealth as an international person and the legislator for this country on the topics committed to it by the Constitution. I shall mention s 109 when dealing with what the Constitution provides and to this I now turn.

Because the Constitution creates a Federal Commonwealth, the Parliament of the Commonwealth has a portion of the total legislative powers possessed in sum by the parliaments of the entire country. Power is shared. Also, since the Constitution created the Commonwealth as a federal state, it had to define what legislative power the Federal Parliament should be given, what its executive power should be and who should have that power, and what legislative powers the States should have. It was decided, as well, that the Constitution should itself deal with the Federal judicial power and not leave that to be dealt with by the parliament alone. In this last respect the example followed was that of the Constitution of the United States.

The Constitution apportions legislative power by nominating the topics in respect of which the Federal Parliament might pass laws and by providing that in cases of conflict between State and Federal laws the Federal law should prevail to the extent of the inconsistency (s 109). The power of the State Parliaments and the Constitutions of the various States were, subject to the Constitution, to continue as at the establishment of the Commonwealth, or as at the admission of new States, or as at that State Parliament's establishment until altered in accordance with the Constitution of the State (s 106). The powers of the State Parliaments, unless exclusively vested in the Federal Parliament or withdrawn from the State Parliament, were to continue as at the establishment of the Commonwealth (s 107), and the laws in force in the States were, subject to the Constitution, to continue in force as they were at the establishment of the Commonwealth, even though those laws were on topics given to the Federal Parliament, until that parliament legislated (s 108). The Federal Parliament consists of the Queen, the Senate and the House of Representatives; the Senate is composed of senators for each State directly chosen by the people of the State voting, subject to any law the Federal Parliament should later make, as one electorate. There were originally to be six senators for each State but parliament might increase or diminish the number of members for the States provided equality was maintained for all Original States.

The House of Representatives is composed of members directly chosen by the people of the Commonwealth, the number of whom should as nearly as practicable be twice the number of Senators.

The members of each State are to be in proportion to the respective numbers of their people, but each Original State should have at least five members. The parliament has power to increase or diminish the number of members of the Representatives, but that is subject to the requirement that they should be as nearly as practicable no more than twice the number of the Senators. Provision is made for Senators to have a six-year term with half retiring in each Senate following a dissolution of the Senate (which can occur only upon a double dissolution in the event of a disagreement between the Houses, that the procedure for reaching agreement set out in s 57 of the Constitution could not resolve). The term of the Representatives is three years and no longer, unless that House is earlier dissolved by the Governor-General (s 28). The Senate is to have a President chosen by the Senators (s 17) and the Representatives a Speaker also chosen by the members (s 35). I shall not attempt to summarise the provisions made for elections, nor the qualifications of senators and members of the Representatives, which the curious may discover in those portions of Parts II, III and IV with which I have not dealt.

Federal executive power is vested in the Queen and is exercisable by the Governor-General as her representative. There is a Federal Executive Council to advise the Governor General in the government of the Commonwealth (ss 61, 62 and 64). The Governor-General appoints members of the parliament to administer the departments of State who are to be "the Queen's Ministers of State for the Commonwealth." These sections write responsible government into the Constitution.[2] The executive power extends to the execution and maintenance of the Constitution and the laws of the parliament and comprises those powers deriving from the existence of the Commonwealth and its character as a polity, including its capacity to engage in enterprises and activities peculiarly adapted to the government of a nation and which cannot otherwise be carried on for the benefit of the nation; it extends to matters such as expending money on inquiries, investigations and advocacy in relation to matters affecting public health, and to all activities and functions appropriate to the national government.[3] There is an express power, legislative and executive, to appoint and remove public servants [ss 51(xxxvi), 67].

The Federal judicial power is vested in the High Court of Australia and in such other Federal Courts as the parliament creates (s 71). The High Court has an original jurisdiction and an unlimited appellate jurisdiction from judgments, decrees, orders and sentences of its own single justices, all Federal Courts, the Supreme Courts of the States and from any other court of a State from which at the establishment of the Commonwealth an appeal lay to the Queen in Council (s 73). There is now no appeal from the Supreme Courts of the States to the Privy Council (*Australia Act* 1986, s 11) nor, except with leave of the High Court, upon a question of the limits inter se of Commonwealth and State powers or of those of two or more States, from the High Court (s 74). The original jurisdiction under the Constitution of the High Court is upon the five subject matters listed in s 75, but parliament might confer jurisdiction upon all Federal Courts upon the subject matters listed in s 76 and upon Federal Courts other than the High Court upon the topics in s 75 as well. It may invest State Courts with Federal jurisdiction upon those nine subject matters and, subject to a number of exceptions, has done so.[4] Federal jurisdiction extends to the whole of a controversy of which a Federal claim is a substantial part, even though that remainder is not a Federal claim or claims.[5] This doctrine and the Commonwealth and State cross-vesting legislation have removed from Federal jurisdiction most of its former uncertainty and technicality to the considerable advantage of litigants. Questions of jurisdiction, once the bane of Federal jurisdiction, now rarely arise and, if they do, may easily be resolved by removal to an appropriate State Court. Naturally, the Constitution enables the parliament to appoint the judges and staff necessary to the functioning of Federal Courts.

The legislative powers of the Commonwealth Parliament consist of the concurrent powers itemised in s 51(i)-51(xxxix) of the Constitution; the exclusive powers in relation to the seat of government of the Commonwealth; places acquired by the Commonwealth for public purposes; matters relating to any department of the public service which the Constitution transferred to the Executive Government of the Commonwealth; and other matters declared by the Constitution to be within the parliament's exclusive power, such as the imposition of customs and excise and the power to grant bounties on the production or export of goods, and territory of a State surrendered to and accepted by the Commonwealth (s 52, 90 and 111); those implied from its existence such as the power of self protection[6] and from its character as a nation.[7]

I shall mention some of the more important powers of s 51. They are: trade and commerce overseas and interstate; taxation; borrowing money on the public credit of the Commonwealth; postal, telegraphic, telephonic and other like services (which include television); defence; banking, except State banking, the incorporation of banks and the issue of paper money; insurance except State insurance; bankruptcy, copyright, patents and trademarks; the corporations power, marriage, divorce; invalid, old age and widows' pensions, sickness, pharmaceutical and hospital benefits, and medical and dental services; immigration; external affairs and the acquisition on just terms of property for any purpose for which the Commonwealth can legislate. The trade and commerce, corporations, banking and insurance powers enable the parliament to impose customs and excise duties, particularly aided by the taxation power; to regulate the import and export of goods, for example the export of rutile from Fraser Island;[8] to regulate the trading activities of companies by means of the *Trade Practices Act* 1974 (Cth); and generally to control internal and external commerce. The supply of credit by banks can be and is regulated and life insurance and other forms of insurance are subject to Commonwealth laws. By means of the external affairs power, laws such as the *Racial Discrimination Act* 1975 (Cth) have been passed and the Franklin Dam was prohibited,[9] in each case because treaties and international conventions had been entered into which were held to justify the laws banning domestic activities inconsistent with Australia's treaty obligations. Since the heads or topics of power mentioned in s 51 are given to the national legislature they are interpreted by the High Court "with all the generality which the words used admit".[10] The Court will not concern itself, at least as a general rule, with the object which the legislation seeks to achieve if what it prohibits or allows falls within one or more of the heads of power. Thus, when the export of all minerals and any substances produced in the course of processing or treating them was prohibited without the written approval of the Minister of State for Minerals and Energy, the only question to be decided was whether the trade and commerce power permitted the prohibition of the export of goods. This it manifestly did and if that power was exercised with the object of preserving the environment of Fraser Island, it remained nonetheless a prohibition of the export of goods and was valid for that reason. These principles are applied to all Commonwealth legislative powers except such as are purposive in nature in the sense that pursuit by the law of the constitutional purpose is a condition of the power. The defence power is commonly taken to be one such purposive power.

The Constitution forbids the imposition by the States of duties of customs or excise or of protectionist duties upon interstate trade. Nor may the States without consent of the Commonwealth raise any naval or military force (ss 90 and 114) nor coin any money (s 115) nor subject any "Subject of the Queen, resident in any State" to any disability or discrimination were he or she not a resident of that State (s 117). Such in outline is what the Constitution is and what it provides, at least as I understand it.

Constitutional Change

Sir Maurice Byers
Sir Harry Gibbs

FISCAL IMBALANCE: EXCISE DUTIES

Sir Maurice Byers

I think there are some changes which could be made. The inability of the States to impose a tax which may be a duty of excise is difficult now to justify. What a duty of excise has become, to say the least, is far from clear. It verges on the absurd that a State may not levy a sales tax on goods, but may impose licensing fees based on the quantity or value of past transactions.[1] It is apparent from s 90 of the Constitution that what was intended to be given exclusively to the Commonwealth were those duties of excise which the colonies imposed in association with their duties of customs, that is, a customs duty upon interstate goods and a reduced duty on locally produced goods of the same kind.[2] Whatever a duty of excise now may be[3] it certainly does not bear the meaning contemplated by s 90. It should no longer be within the exclusive power of the Commonwealth to impose duties of excise.

Sir Harry Gibbs

I am in complete accord with the view of Sir Maurice, that it should no longer be within the exclusive power of the Commonwealth to impose duties of excise. Although, as Sir Maurice has suggested, it seems apparent from s 90 of the Constitution that it was intended that there should be a close connection between duties of excise and duties of customs, some High Court judges have thought that the section was intended to have a wider economic purpose and have accordingly given the words of the section a meaning much wider than its connection with custom duty would suggest. Unfortunately, there has been no agreement as to what the wider purpose is, and the effect of the section remains obscure. As two members of the High Court themselves have said, "the quest for a constitutional purpose has proved to be almost as contentious as the quest for a meaning of the text has been elusive."[4] The decisions seem to give the section a quite capricious effect. State taxes on the sale and production of goods have been held to be duties of excise,[5] but licence fees calculated by reference to sales and purchases made in a period other than the licence period have been held not to be excises when imposed in relation to the sale of tobacco or alcohol,[6] although they have been held to be excises when imposed in relation to the processing of fish or the slaughtering of meat.[7] Stamp duties imposed on receipts of payments on sales have been held to be excises[8] and so has a fee for operating a gas and oil pipeline,[9] although the fee was not calculated by reference to the amount of gas or oil carried. The invalidation of State imposts of this kind does not significantly assist the Commonwealth to control the economy, but it seriously limits the capacity of the States to raise money by taxation. The States are forced to impose taxes, such as payroll tax and taxes on financial dealings, which from an economic point of view are much less satisfactory than sales taxes would be. There is pending before the High Court at present a case in which the effect of s 90 has been argued again.[10] The decision may remove some of the uncertainty from the section, but it is too much to hope that it can remove all its disadvantages. On the other hand, it could make them worse. Clearly it would be desirable to amend s 90 to allow the States to impose duties of excise.

FISCAL IMBALANCE: TIED GRANTS

Sir Harry Gibbs

There is another section of the Constitution which has thrown out of balance the relations between the Commonwealth and the States. That is s 96, which enables the parliament to grant financial assistance to any State on such terms and conditions as the parliament thinks fit. Judicial decisions on this section have established that there is no limitation on the nature of the terms and conditions that may be imposed and that a grant of financial assistance will be valid, although the conditions on which it is made require a State to apply the money for a purpose in relation to which the Commonwealth has no power to legislate directly and which would otherwise be the sole responsibility of the State.[11] For example, the Constitution does not give the Commonwealth any power with regard to the provision of roads, education, housing or legal aid, but grants are made to the States to be applied for those purposes in accordance with detailed conditions laid down by the Commonwealth. There are some advantages in this system. It strengthens the Commonwealth's control of the economy (if that is an advantage) and it enables national policies to be given effect. There are however grave disadvantages. Firstly the financial relations between the Commonwealth and the States have been thrown out of joint. The Commonwealth raises more than 75 percent of all taxes levied in Australia, although its expenditure only represents about 50 percent of all governmental expenditure. The States have to rely on Commonwealth grants for about 55 percent of their revenue. In other words, the Commonwealth raises many millions of dollars more than it needs for its own constitutional purposes and the States raise much less than they need for their purposes. State governments are thus rendered less able to control their own affairs and find it more difficult to plan for the future. At the same time the system leads to a lack of accountability since the Commonwealth raises money but is not responsible for the way in which all of it is spent, whereas the States spend money without being responsible for the manner in which it is raised. This imbalance between financial responsibility and financial resources appears to be greater in Australia than in any other federation.

The situation could be remedied by agreement between the Commonwealth and the States, but experience does not give much ground for hope in that direction. Constitutional change to solve the problem would be desirable, but it has to be said that it is very difficult to suggest an amendment which would be both effective and acceptable.

FAMILIES

Sir Maurice Byers

There is no good reason why the marriage power should not allow the passing of laws with respect to the children in the household of a married couple whether or not they are the biological children of the married couple. Legislative attempts to achieve this have been held to be invalid.[12]

Sir Harry Gibbs

I agree that it would seem sensible that the power of the Commonwealth to deal with the custody, guardianship and maintenance of infants should be extended to include children living in the household of a married couple, even though the children are not the biological children of the married couple.

THE ECONOMY

Sir Maurice Byers

There is much to be said for the view that the Commonwealth, now that there is truly an Australian economy, should be given an express power to pass laws with respect to it and should no longer be confined to its taxing and banking powers in order to regulate it.

Sir Harry Gibbs

This suggestion that Sir Maurice makes, that the Commonwealth should be given express power to pass laws with respect to the economy, is important. It is certainly arguable that the Commonwealth should have clear power to regulate the Australian economy, although perhaps the argument is one that might be resolved better by economists than by lawyers. However, if the argument were accepted, I would suggest that great care would have to be taken in framing the words conferring the necessary power.

CENTRAL GOVERNMENT POWER

Sir Harry Gibbs

This raises a question that goes to the heart of the relations between the Commonwealth and the various States. The Constitution was framed on the principle that the powers of the Commonwealth, although wide, would be defined and limited, whereas the powers of the States would remain undefined, so that any power not given to the Commonwealth should remain vested in the parliaments of the several States. It was of course recognised that there might be concurrent exercises of power, so that the laws of the Commonwealth and the laws of a State might conflict, and, as Sir Maurice has mentioned, provision was made for the laws of the Commonwealth to prevail if that occurred.

However, some of the powers of the Commonwealth have been given an undefined and unlimited scope by the interpretation that the High Court has given to them. This is particularly true of the power to legislate with regard to external affairs. The ordinary citizen might be surprised to be told that under the power to make laws with respect to external affairs, the Commonwealth Parliament can pass a law that would prevent the construction of a dam in the centre of Tasmania,[13] or a law that would render it unlawful for a State minister to refuse consent to the purchase of a Crown Lease of land in North Queensland.[14] However, legislation of the Commonwealth has been held to have those effects, because it has been passed to give effect to an international treaty. The results of this interpretation, which I would suggest are harmful to Federation, although Sir Maurice might not agree, are twofold. First, the scope of the power of the Commonwealth can in effect be extended by executive action, for the Commonwealth Government, by arranging to enter into a treaty, can give the parliament a foothold to exercise the external affairs power by legislating to implement the treaty. Secondly, the result is that the scope of this power of the Commonwealth Parliament is no longer limited and defined, but is, on the contrary, vague and undefined. It encroaches on the power of the States, so that for instance both the Commonwealth and a State can regulate the carrying out of forestry operations within a State, with resulting conflict and duplication of governmental activity.

To interpret Commonwealth powers in this way involves a striking departure from the principle that the Commonwealth has defined powers and from the further principle that under the Constitution the States are not bodies subordinate to the Commonwealth, but are independent within the areas of power not granted to the Commonwealth. Thus although I agree that there is quite a strong case for extending some Commonwealth powers, any new powers should be defined and limited, so that they do not allow the Commonwealth to enter into literally every aspect of State activity. At the same time power such as that with regard to external affairs should be limited to prevent this wholesale intrusion by the Commonwealth into the affairs of the States.

RESERVE POWERS AND ELECTORAL SYSTEM

Sir Maurice Byers

But there are as well more central questions raised by the Constitution. Many take the view that Chapter II of the Constitution (the Executive Government) deals only with the historical as opposed to the real nature of the State. By its real nature I mean that the executive power vested in the Queen and exercisable by the Governor-General as her representative is only exercisable on Ministerial advice. The only exception to that is the appointment of the Prime Minister following an election when there has, at least in theory, ceased to be a Prime Minister to tender advice even if it be only as to the choice of his successor. And it cannot be denied that the language of the Constitution on this central question of constitutional law is elliptical in the extreme. It seems to me that one must read the provisions of s 62 relating to the Federal Executive Council which is to advise the Governor-General in the government of the Commonwealth as requiring him or her to act only on that advice and never to act without it (save in the case I have mentioned) and never without exception to act against it. The system of responsible government which we undoubtedly do have — by reason of the Constitution and history — commits the real exercise of executive power to the Cabinet who must answer for it to the parliament. Sir Samuel Griffith said of them:

> They are therefore called Responsible Ministers. If they do wrong, they can be punished or dismissed from office without affecting any change in the Headship of the State. Revolution is therefore no longer a possibility — for a change of Ministers affects peacefully the desired result... The present form of development of responsible government is that, when the branch of the Legislature which more immediately represents the people disapproves of the actions of Ministers, or ceases to have confidence in them, the Head of State dismisses them, or accepts their resignation, and appoints new ones.[15]

In such a system there is no room for autocratic power in the Crown whether by way of reserve powers or otherwise. The view I take is undoubtedly a minority one and, if so, there exists strong reason to write into the Constitution the real system of government.

At the same time the uncertainty, which the present electoral system guarantees, should be addressed. The electoral system produces a House of Representatives controlled by one party and a Senate controlled either by that party's opposition or by whatever combination of two parties that circumstances may create. Since the Senate, save for its inability to "originate" an appropriation or tax bill or to amend them, has equal power with the House of Representatives in respect of all proposed laws (s 53) the possibility of a refusal of supply always exists. Experience should have taught us that this is undesirable, and that the Senate should give way, just as the House of Lords and most Upper Houses must.

Sir Harry Gibbs

Chapter II of the Constitution, which deals with Executive Power, would undoubtedly be misleading to a reader who lacked a knowledge of constitutional history, as I am afraid a good many readers do nowadays. That is because the actual wording of the provisions is governed by conventions which are not expressed in the written words of the Constitution. Those conventions have undergone a good deal of development in the United Kingdom since the 17th century and in Australia since the colonies became self-governing. They are not rules of law and according to an important Canadian decision[16] are not enforceable by the courts. However, they are rules which the monarch and her representatives, who by tradition must be quite divorced from politics, habitually observe. They would not, of their own force, necessarily govern the acts of a President under a Republican system. One could see that there is something to be said for achieving a greater certainty by writing the conventions into the Constitution. There are, however, strong arguments against that course. First, it should be remembered that a written Constitution is inevitably a small part of the whole body of constitutional principles — the written Constitution is perhaps the tip of the constitutional iceberg. If the conventions were written into the Constitution, the High Court would have the power to decide what they require and would have power to enforce them. In a political crisis, the delay and uncertainty resulting from litigation could paralyse government. One circumstance in which the conventions allow the representative of the Queen to act other than on ministerial advice has been mentioned by Sir Maurice, and that is the appointment of a Prime Minister following an election. With great respect, I do not agree that that is the only such circumstance, but it will serve as a sufficient example.

Suppose, following an election, no party had a majority in parliament. That can easily occur; it is the case in New South Wales at present and was the case in Tasmania in 1989. The Governor General would then have to decide whom to commission as Prime Minister, and if his decision could be tested in the courts, the absence of a government in the meantime could result in chaos. I should add that in my opinion there are other situations in which the Governor

General can exercise the reserve powers or, in other words, in which convention allows him or her to act without ministerial advice or contrary to ministerial advice. One such situation would arise if a government having been denied supply was attempting to govern without supply.

Sir Maurice has referred to the fact that the Senate can reject an appropriation bill or a bill imposing taxation, although it cannot amend such bills. In most places where the Constitution is modelled on that of Westminster, the upper house has no power to reject an appropriation bill. The position is quite different under the system of government in the United States. There is certainly a strong argument in favour of depriving the Senate of its power to reject an appropriation bill, although the Senate itself might oppose any such change. However, the position may arguably be different in relation to bills imposing taxation. It is one thing to say that the Senate should not refuse supply when the House of Representatives has granted it, but it does not follow that the Senate should be deprived of the power to prevent the imposition of a particular tax. However, if the Constitution were to be revised, these questions would require detailed consideration.

BILL OF RIGHTS

Sir Harry Gibbs

There is one other possible change to the Constitution, to which Sir Maurice has not referred, perhaps because he does not recommend it, but which I should like to mention, because it is so often advocated. That is the suggestion that a Bill of Rights be written into the Constitution. At first sight, it might seem attractive to have a constitutional guarantee of basic rights notwithstanding the fact that Australia is one of the comparatively few countries where basic rights are generally respected. There are, however, some powerful arguments against adopting a constitutional Bill of Rights. One is that to do so would have an adverse effect on the judiciary. The application of the very general words of a Bill of Rights inevitably requires judges to decide matters of policy that would best be decided by the legislature. Thus, the provision that no one should be deprived of life, liberty or property without due process of law has been regarded in the United States, Canada and Germany as empowering judges to decide upon the validity of laws which either prohibit or permit abortion, and the results reached by the judges have been neither consistent nor satisfying either to those who strongly oppose abortion or to those who strongly support the right to abortion. When judges are required to decide political questions, public respect for their impartiality is diminished and the temptation to stack the bench with judges whose views seem acceptable to the government becomes irresistible, as American experience has shown. The flow of litigation that results from attempts to invoke a Bill of Rights greatly increases the work load of the courts, which are already creaking under the strain. The effect that the courts give to provisions of this kind is utterly unpredictable. The decisions under s 92 of our Constitution, which provides that trade, commerce and intercourse amongst the States should be absolutely free, shows how apparently simple words can acquire a variety of meanings during the course of judicial interpretation.

The effect which courts in other countries have given to Bills of Rights sometimes seems to impede the course of justice rather than to advance it. May I give a couple of examples? In the United States, the words of the Fifth Amendment that no one "shall be compelled in any criminal case to be a witness against himself" have been held to mean that any person taken into custody must be informed of his or her right to consult counsel. In one case where a person was convicted of murder, the evidence implicating the accused included the facts that he had informed the police that he could take them to the place where the murdered girl was buried, that he had taken them there and that they had found the body. That was in 1968. When the case reached the Supreme Court in 1977, it was held that the conviction should be quashed because the accused had not been informed of his right to consult counsel.[17] There was a new trial at which evidence was given of the finding of the body, but not that the accused had directed police to it. The accused was again convicted. After some fluctuations of judicial opinion, the matter reached the Supreme Court again in 1984. This time the conviction was affirmed.[18] It is difficult to see what useful purpose the Bill of Rights served in that case.

The same may be said of a New Zealand decision quashing the conviction of a driver given a breath test, which showed an excess of alcohol in the blood, but who had not been warned of his right to consult a lawyer.[19] The advice of a lawyer would not have proved very useful because it would have been an offence to refuse to take the breath test.

There are other disadvantages in the incorporation of a Bill of Rights into a constitution. One is that the concentration on the rights of one person leads to the restriction of the rights, liberty or reasonable expectations of another. For example, to insist on a right to freedom of expression in the press would be to threaten the right to or expectation of individual privacy. It is already alarming to see how reliance is placed on legislation designed to prevent the discrimination against certain groups in our society as a justification for demands for the restriction of the freedom of speech when utterances are made which are critical of the members of a protected group. Added to these and other disadvantages is the fact that the existence of a Bill of Rights would not necessarily prevent the wholesale denial of basic rights. Yugoslavia, for instance, had a Bill of Rights. One constitutional change we do not need is the inclusion of a Bill of Rights into the Constitution.

SUMMARY

Sir Harry Gibbs

To sum up, I agree with Sir Maurice that some changes to the Constitution would be desirable. We are not in complete agreement as to the nature of those changes. I do agree, however, that none of the changes which he has suggested or which I have suggested could be called a matter of life and death. Our Constitution is not perfect, but it works reasonably well.

Sir Maurice Byers

The alterations I have suggested are not matters of life and death, but they are desirable. In particular, despite the innocent faith of many political parties in an apparently unrestrained and unguided economy, a power to curb the damage it may inflict upon Australian citizens is necessary lest economic unpredictability wreck grievous harm upon all, as it has upon our primary producers, whose situation, in the scramble for markets, is likely to grow worse and that of this country as a whole.

COMMENTARY

CONSIDERATION OF A BILL OF RIGHTS

Dennis Mahoney (Judge of the NSW Court of Appeal)

The form of the Constitution must depend ultimately on what you want it to do. It is worth commenting here on (a) the control of the exercise of government power, and (b) what form of Constitution is best adapted to producing wealth for Australia.

The exercise of government power causes one a good deal of concern in these times. The first point about power is that the exercise of government power and the extent of it is something which is becoming a matter for increasing concern. The government can and does exercise power in an extraordinary number of ways that are intrusive into the ordinary life of the individual. One could give examples at length. For example, the extent of the power of the Commonwealth, and the extent to which it has been exercised in the supervision of monetary transactions, is frightening. Those who have seen the legislation concerned with the reporting by banks and other institutions of what a person does with sums over $10,000 these days can only be alarmed. It is chilling when one contemplates what effect this can have upon the vesting of power and knowledge in a bureaucracy. And of course the availability of computer techniques for automatic transfer of information of this kind must be borne in mind.

The second point about power is there now seem to be few if any moral constraints on government in the exercise of legislative or constitutional power. In former times one could be confident that a government, although it had power to do such and such, would not do it. "The public would not stand for it." Experience has shown that there are very few things that the public will not stand for these days; few things that they will know of and take steps to prevent.

Thirdly, power, when it is given for one purpose, is very often exercised for a completely different purpose. Sir Harry and Sir Maurice have referred to the use by government of the External Affairs power. It is clear that, on occasions, treaties have been made for one purpose but the powers derived from them have been exercised for a completely different purpose. And yet, that has not brought down a government. It has passed in and out of courts with no more interest than the quizzical scrutiny of lawyers.

My argument is that the control of the exercise of power today is a matter of importance. Accordingly, in considering the form of a Constitution and any amendments that are to be made, this should be right at the head of the list. We should consider what the Constitution now does and what it should or should not do in that regard; what restraints should be placed upon the exercise of power. The existence of federalism is, of course, the fundamental and traditional method of controlling the exercise of power.

The enactment of some form of human rights guarantee in the Constitution is very important. The time has come when we cannot assume that a government under the particular pressures of the day would not see it expedient, or in their view necessary, to do things which fundamentally infringe important human rights guarantees. The real problem is not that the government will infringe human rights for sinister purposes, but that they will try to do it for purposes which the bureaucracy will advise them are good at that particular time. If we do not have human rights guarantees enacted at that moment, we shall never have them. Human right guarantees must be enacted before we need them: if we wait until we need them, they will not then be enacted. So it is important that in any consideration of the form of a constitution we need a wide-ranging review of matters such as these.

COMMENTARY

THE POSSIBILITY OF AN ABORIGINAL TREATY

Q

What is the constitutional power under which the Federal Government could negotiate and sign a treaty with the Aboriginals?

Sir Maurice Byers

I do not think there is any express power to do so, and on the other hand I do not see why you could not say the executive power would extend to that. What effect you could give to it would be another question.

HOW CONSTITUTIONAL CHANGE IS INSTIGATED

Q (to Sir Maurice)

I did not quite understand your explanation of changing the Constitution. It has been put to me that our Constitution is an Act of the British Parliament, and to do away with the Monarchy or reserve power or whatever would need an Act of the British Parliament.

Sir Maurice Byers

One of the sections of the Constitution, s 128, enables the Constitution to be changed by vote or referendum, with which everyone is familiar. It has been successful on eight occasions. The success rate is not high, but the Constitution has been changed in a number of ways. The language of s 128 does not seem to me to be inconsistent with a constitutional change which would replace the Queen as the person who is the constitutional Head of State, with a President, who would be Constitutional Head of State. Those changes are within the competence of the Australian people. They would have, of course, to achieve the constitutional majorities to be effective, but the United Kingdom Parliament has no longer any power to legislate in respect of Australia. It would be highly doubtful in my view that it had that power in 1985, in the sense that it would be difficult to imagine that against the will of Australians, the United Kingdom Parliament could pass a law effective in Australia changing the Constitution. That is just unbelievable. Or that if they did, it could be of effect here, particularly bearing in mind the effect of s 128, which says that the Constitution may only be changed in the relevant fashion.

Q

In the United States, a number of States provide to the people a mechanism, which I think in California is known as a proposition, in which with 50,000 names you can raise a proposition which becomes a referendum. Do either of the speakers think this technique would have any merit in the changing of our Constitution in order to provide greater power to the people?

Sir Harry Gibbs

No. On the contrary, the procedure has proved highly inconvenient. For example, in the United States a proposition to restrict the taxing powers of the legislature was enthusiastically carried, and the result of it made it very difficult for the government of the State affected to govern.

Sir Maurice Byers

I must say in this respect I totally agree with what Sir Harry has said. I think it is a lot of nonsense.

Margaret Beazley

The Constitution is a dynamic and living organism which needs much better understanding by the population as a whole if we are to have any sensible debate as to the type of government we are going to have next century.

IV

BRAVE NEW REPUBLIC

INTRODUCTION

Kim Santow

One of the paradoxes about constitutional discussion is that the Constitution is meant to represent (to quote Sir Maurice Byers) the sentiment of a people behind the idea of nationhood. Yet it is extraordinarily difficult to find people who can describe it in a way that is intelligible to us all. I well remember a line in HG Wells' *The History of Mr Polly*.[1] This described a scene as like "a very beautiful thing seen through the smoke of a passing train". The Constitution may well be that very beautiful thing.

We are fortunate that Dr Saunders is not only a distinguished academic, but well able to communicate in a way that is intelligible to us all. She penetrates the passing smoke so we actually see the shape of the Republican train as it races towards the year 2001. We may not know until 2001 what kind of republic it will be, but Dr Saunders' remarks will give us insight.

A Republican Model: Would More be Better Than Less?

Cheryl Saunders[*]

This chapter is about the form which the model for an Australian republic might take, rather than about whether we should move to a republic at all. The model is much the more difficult issue and at least as important. I think it is obvious that sooner or later Australia will break its links with the Crown. The only real question is when. The centenary of Federation in 2001 is a symbolic date and for that reason may be the most appropriate. It implies nothing about our relationship with Britain, and makes no judgement about the monarch in person. It simply marks a stage in our own constitutional history.

---

[*] Please note: my views are not necessarily those of the Constitutional Centenary Foundation or any of its members. There is a wide variety of opinions on most constitutional issues within the Foundation. That is one of its major strengths. But Foundation members are committed to the open expression of those views in the interests of a wide-ranging and informed public debate on the constitutional system of Australia in the decade leading to the centenary of Federation in 2001.

But if not on our own initiative, then or at some other time, I would expect us eventually to become a republic through the evolution of the Commonwealth (using that term to mean the former British Commonwealth) itself. The relationship between the Crown and the member countries of the Commonwealth has already gone through a series of major changes, reflecting changes in the status and perceived needs of the countries themselves. In the case of Australia, for example:

- In 1901 the Governor-General appointed to represent the Queen under the new Constitution was recognised as an agent of the British Government and accountable to it on important matters.
- Within 25 years, this was completely changed. In 1926 the Imperial Conference accepted that the Crown and the representative of the Crown acted on the advice of the government of the relevant country only, in dealing with that country's affairs. The impetus for the change came from events in Canada, but the principle applied to all the other countries involved (called, at that time, Dominions).
- In 1930 the Imperial Conference agreed that the King would appoint the Governor-General on the advice of the Dominion Government even if he was personally opposed to the choice. This time the impetus came from Australia, following the famous struggle between Prime Minister Scullin and the King over the appointment of the first Australian Governor-General, Isaac Isaacs. Again, however, the principle applied to all Dominions.
- In 1953 the Royal title was changed to enable each country to adopt a form suitable to its own circumstances, in addition to an element common to all.
- In 1973 the royal style and titles were changed again in Australia to recognise the Queen as the Queen of Australia.
- In 1986 the *Australia Acts* (Cth and UK) formally recognised that the Queen would perform no functions in relation to any part of Australia except to appoint or dismiss her representatives, or, perhaps, when she was personally present in Australia.

Most other Commonwealth countries have followed the same path from colonial status to independence during this period. A majority of them became republics over the same period as well, although the largest countries, including Australia and Canada, so far have retained links with the Crown. The next major phase for the Commonwealth as a whole may well be recognition of the Queen as the Head of the Commonwealth alone, with all individual member countries selecting and appointing their own Heads of State.

Such a development would be consistent with what is happening in the world at large. The pace of international activity and interchange is far greater than ever before. The description of the world as a global village is rapidly coming true. In such an environment, Heads of State are likely to be pressed into service increasingly for international as well as national purposes. Inevitably, each country will wish to have its own Head of State, serving its individual needs. The advantage of this arrangement is likely to be as obvious for Britain itself as for the other members of the Commonwealth which presently share the Queen. To put it simply, the royal family may simply not have time to act as Head of State for 15 Commonwealth countries.

If I am right about this, discussion of the republican model becomes even more important. It may be not only timely but urgent to think about the changes we would want to make to the constitutional system if Australia broke its links with the Crown.

There is a view abroad that this is too technical a matter to be of much interest to the Australian people. The assumption is that it is rather a matter for governments and politicians. I disagree. The situation we are presently in is not unlike the end of last century when there was wide support for Federation but much greater uncertainty about what sort of federation to have. The people made up their minds on that occasion, after an unusually popular process. They will have to make up their minds again, if the Constitution is effectively to be changed. For that reason, if for no other, the people will need to understand and approve a republican model. But there is another reason. Discussion of the model for a republic offers a positive opportunity to develop active popular interest in and support for the new structures. To use the modern jargon, people should be able to feel that they "own" the republican constitution. If we manage to achieve that, the benefits will be felt beyond republicanism, by the rest of the constitutional system. But any such process will take time. The opportunity will be wasted if we rush it.

In this chapter I will consider the position of the Head of State as a discrete part of the constitutional system as far as possible. I do not wish to exaggerate the extent to which that can be done. The position of Head of State is closely bound up with the political process. The structures of parliament and government historically were shaped by their association with the Crown. In my view, both must be included in the republican debate to some degree.

But there is no need to get into other broad constitutional issues. The operation of the federal system, for example, is strictly irrelevant, although, if I may digress, it seems to me essential that any republican model includes States as well as the Commonwealth. There is also, of course, a separate set of questions about how the link with the Crown may be accomplished at the State level and the models which each of the States might create.

Other constitutional questions, such as the protection of individual rights and the structure and operation of courts similarly are not directly relevant to republicanism, using the term in this relatively narrow sense. That is not to say that these issues should not be considered over the decade. On the contrary, the Constitutional Centenary Foundation (the Foundation) firmly believes that they should. If, following debate, we decided that a range of changes should be made, we might combine them in a larger constitutional package by 2001. But there is no necessary connection between republicanism in the sense of breaking the links with the Crown and some of these other broad constitutional issues.

Can we become a republic so that more is not lost than gained by change? My short answer is "yes". I would hope that we can improve on current arrangements. But to do so we must be prepared to take a clear look at the present constitutional system; honestly identify its strengths and weaknesses; put aside partisan differences in the interests of an informed debate; and think creatively and constructively about the changes that are needed.

The starting point is the present. There is no doubt that the British constitutional monarchy has been a remarkably flexible, adaptable and sensitive institution. As it has evolved over the last century the office of the Head of State has been perceived to transcend the political process, enabling incumbents to speak to and for the community as a whole. At the same time, however, the Crown exercises almost no actual power. Effective control lies with the government drawn from a democratically elected parliament. The very few exceptions apply in extreme emergency cases, where the Crown may act without advice, in the exercise of "reserve" powers. The very lack of definition of these imposes a discipline on governments and ensures that the powers, in Britain at least, are never used. These arrangements have evolved over the centuries almost by accident. Partly for this reason and partly because the rules are so elusive, they depend largely on constitutional convention rather than law.

The institution of constitutional monarchy, with those advantages more or less intact, has been inherited by countries like Australia, which retain the Queen as the formal Head of State with Governors-General or State Governors as her representatives. To all intents and purposes the representatives of the Crown are the actual Heads of State. In Australia, the system offers the same combination of formal power vested in the Crown with actual control by the government of the day. The same conventions apply and the same uncertainties about them exist. The aura which the office has acquired from association with the Crown affects the position of the Crown's representatives also. In addition, the constitutional monarchy has proved for Australia an extremely convenient way of appointing a Head of State. The actual choice is that of the Prime Minister. But the formality of appointment by the Queen, coupled with the procedures necessarily involved, has some influence on appointments, a clear influence on removals and adds a certain mystique to the entire procedure.

Nevertheless, the institution is far from perfect.

- In the countries making up Great Britain, the process of transition from a more or less absolute monarch to an absolutely sovereign parliament shifted the power from the Crown to parliament and thus effectively to the government but prevented express recognition of popular sovereignty or consideration of its significance for the constitutional system. In the words of one United States observer, the result was government of the people for the people but not necessarily by the people. This same characteristic is reflected in our own Constitution. It may be one of the reasons for the relative lack of public interest in it.

- The conventions which worked pretty well in Great Britain work rather less well here. The reasons are complex. They include our written Constitution and the differences in our political culture as it has evolved. The fact that the Governor-General holds office for a term and that the office itself is not in jeopardy if an ill-judged or poorly accepted decision is made is another influencing factor. One result is a tendency on the part of governments to put too much pressure on the office of Head of State rather than accepting responsibility for the advice that is given.
- The principles and structures associated with the constitutional monarchy are even more opaque and obscure in Australia than in Britain. While this makes for flexibility, it also makes the constitutional system hard to understand. And it has a tendency to confuse the lines of accountability for decisions that are made.

In constructing a republican model, I assume we are seeking to do three things:

- Preserve the advantages of the existing system as far as possible.
- Improve on the disadvantages, again as far as possible.
- Create a system suitable to meet new needs and pressures on it.

All sorts of issues need to be dealt with. How to appoint the Head of State is an obvious one, which has already received some public attention. But the key to them all is to ask: what sort of Head of State do we want? And what do we want the Head of State to do? The first is easier to answer than the second. I suspect that we may want to preserve the aspect of the constitutional monarchy which provides a Head of State who appears to rise above politics, to embody the Australian community and to present a figure of whom we can be proud on the international scene.

The question of powers is more difficult, however, and potentially contentious. Most of the debate up to now has assumed, in the interests of avoiding controversy, that the powers of the Head of State and the conventions which govern their exercise should be the same under the republic as under the monarchy. The problem is, however, that:

- We cannot assume that the conventions will carry over from the constitutional monarchy to a republican Australia.
- It follows that, on this approach, we need either to spell the conventions out or to provide a way for that to be done.
- If we choose the first of those options we need to say what the conventions are — which is no easy matter when we are fundamentally disagreed on some of them. But if we choose the second, we must leave the task of spelling out the conventions to the government or the parliament, which I suspect may be even less palatable.

The question I ask today is whether, before we worry about how to deal with the conventions that govern the exercise of the powers of the Head of State, we should think about the powers themselves.

Many of the existing powers of the Crown relate to the parliament. The powers to call the parliament together, assent to bills, dissolve the parliament, appoint and dismiss governments drawn from the parliament are examples. The relationship between the Crown and parliament does not necessarily have a logical basis which should be preserved for all time. In effect it reflects the state of play when the battles between the Crown and parliament were ended, with victory for the latter. Parliament was supreme, but the Crown was still part of if: assenting to bills, calling the parliament together, dissolving parliament. As responsible government became established, with the principle that the Crown acts in almost all cases on the advice of the government, these powers effectively passed to the government. Governments have a high degree of control of parliaments anyway, under a system of responsible government. But it is not obvious to me that governments need these particular powers. Some of them at least may be able to be exercised in another way, with benefit to the system as a whole.

A REPUBLICAN MODEL

In developing a republican model, it may therefore be productive to think more deeply about the powers of the Head of State. The Head of State should have the powers appropriate to the office as we conceive it. But other powers currently vested in the Crown or the Governor-Generals or Governors may be better exercised by someone else — even the parliament itself, in some cases. It may be that some existing powers are not necessary at all. Assent to legislation may be an example.

Two of the more difficult powers may be used to explore this approach. The first includes the power to summons parliament, to prorogue it and to dissolve it. These powers are vested in the Crown, but almost always exercised on advice. There is some debate about whether the Crown has a discretion to refuse to dissolve when the government has lost the confidence of the Lower House and someone else has the potential to form a government. But it is rare for the government to lose the confidence of the House and even more rare for this to occur in circumstances where someone else could take over.

These powers are a hang-over from a previous era. These days, they confer on the government, rather than on the Crown, the most sweeping powers over the parliament to which it is accountable. They enable the government to dissolve parliament more or less at will. Even more surprisingly, because it is contrary to the very principle on which responsible government rests, they enable the government to prorogue parliament, effectively preventing a vote of no confidence if the parliament were minded to pass one. Why should that be? Only because it once was. Is there any reason why the decision to dissolve or prorogue could not be vested in an absolute majority of the parliament itself? Where the government has the confidence of the Lower House, all this would involve is a motion by the Prime Minister, passed by the House itself. In those rare cases where the government has lost the confidence of the House, the parliament could either adopt the motion or express confidence in another leader who might be commissioned to form a government.

The second example concerns the powers to appoint and dismiss a government. When the Governor-General chooses a new government, following an election, he or she in effect is making a judgment about who can attract the confidence of the House. Usually the decision is obvious, because one party is an outright winner. But in the case of a hung parliament it may be more difficult; and the Crown's decision may be disproved by the House itself. One possibility, in this event, is that the choice of a government after an election might also be left to the parliament. But on balance, I think not: it is convenient for a Head of State to choose a government quickly when the results of an election are announced. Nevertheless the symbolism of responsibility of government to parliament might be preserved by a constitutional requirement for the Head of State to appoint a government which appears most likely to have the confidence of the House, and for the House to ratify that decision as soon as possible thereafter.

The power to dismiss a government raises other, more difficult issues.

There is one circumstance in which exercise of the power is straightforward. The parliamentary system assumes that a government which has the confidence of the Lower House of parliament is entitled to govern. If it loses that confidence it must resign. If a government failed to resign, which would be almost inconceivable, one present fallback is dismissal by the Crown. There is no need to retain this power in the Head of State for this purpose, however. The rule could equally be expressed in a constitution. It would require a more careful statement about what amounts to a vote of no confidence, which might be no bad thing if it freed members of parliament to deliberate with a degree of freedom on other matters.

The controversy arises over whether there are other circumstances in which the Crown can dismiss a government. There are two main precedents in Australia:

- The dismissal of Premier Lang for illegality in 1932.
- The dismissal of the Whitlam Government following rejection of supply by the Senate in 1975.

I remain to be convinced that either of these circumstances justify retention of the power to dismiss by a Head of State. Dismissal on the grounds of illegality is better dealt with by the courts. Rejection of supply seems to me to be the one power which an Upper House should not have, as long as we retain responsible government with its assumption that Lower Houses make and break governments. I acknowledge that there is an underlying concern here that Heads of State and Upper Houses need these powers to deal with governments which go mad or bad. But I make two points:

- Lower Houses are specifically designed to deal with that problem. If they do not do it, we need to do something about Lower Houses or change the system altogether.
- And even if we did need an ultimate fallback, to deal with crises of this kind, neither a Head of State nor an Upper House is sufficiently reliable for the purpose. Upper Houses will never reject Supply if the government has a majority in them. Governments have controlled the Senate from time to time in the past and undoubtedly will do so again. The point is even more obvious at State level. A Head of State is not necessarily qualified and does not have the support staff to make judgments about illegal action on the part of governments. In any event, under the present system, Heads of State effectively are appointed by the leader of the government itself which is hardly a suitable foundation on which to build a safeguard of this kind.

I say all this with some trepidation, because I am aware of the undercurrent of suspicion that the republican debate is a way to get at the powers of the Senate. Certainly that is not my motive. On the contrary, my own view is that the power to reject supply is a distraction to the Senate, properly constituted and resourced as a House of Review. But this analysis only serves to underscore the point I made at the outset, that it is not possible to isolate the republican debate from the operation of the political process. Alteration of the powers of the Senate ideally requires consideration of the role of parliament, its relationship with government, and the functions which each house performs.

This is not the place for an analysis of the rest of the powers of the Crown in relation to parliament. They are dealt with in the Constitutional Centenary Foundation's discussion paper on the role of parliament paper, which should be released soon. It is intended to provide a broad base for discussion about all aspects of the constitutional system, including this one. The Foundation hopes that a wide range of people will be involved in that debate.

In conclusion let me summarise where this approach to developing a republican model might take us. First, I see no reason why we cannot create an office of Head of State which attracts the same respect and affection as does the present office in good times. The important thing is to be clear about what we are seeking to achieve. The method of selection in my view is less important than setting appropriate standards with the first few appointments. My own preference, for what it is worth, is election by a special majority of both Houses of the Commonwealth Parliament to ensure support across political lines. I note, however, current levels of support for direct election. That would be harder to manage, but not impossible.

Secondly, the model would confer only those constitutional functions on the Head of State which have a modern identifiable purpose. The appointment of the Prime Minister following an election is one example. Another may be the exercise on advice of executive power, if the act of giving and receiving advice adds value to the process by giving the Head of State an opportunity to "advise, encourage and warn".

The advantages of this approach to the powers of the Head of State include an enhanced function for parliament; clarification of the real responsibilities of government; elimination of uncertainty and controversy over the reserve powers; and a constitution more readily understood by the people.

Obviously these suggestions would need public discussion and thinking through. They depend on other changes to the political system, including the legislative-executive relationship and the operations of parliament itself. An overhaul of these might in fact be welcomed by the public, if the tenor of recent comment in the media is any guide. I have always been sceptical about the line of reasoning that says that because so many referendums for constitutional change have failed, only the most apparently minor changes will get through. I do not think the people are so silly. But whatever the truth of that assumption for the constitutional debate generally, this may be an occasion when the Australian people would prefer to settle for more rather than less.

Some Remarks about the Republic

Roger Gyles

On the one hand there are those in favour of a republic, and on the other, those against. The question obliges us to compare gains and losses and that inevitably is subjective. Identifying what are gains and what are losses is subjective enough and then the comparison between them is even more subjective. Dr Saunders illustrates the complexity and difficulty of quarantining the republican issue from other very important constitutional questions.

The real issue is whether or not the Queen will remain as Australian Head of State. Those who favour that will do so for a variety of reasons. There will be those who have a genuine commitment to retaining the British link. They would not form a majority of the population, but would be a continuing and important voice. A much larger group, and I include myself in this group, are concerned that unintended consequences will follow from change which appears, at first glance, to be relatively benign and simple; and we are therefore cautious about the change. On the other hand, there can be no denying the strong Irish influence upon those contending that we should break the link with the Crown in alliance with many other parts of the community which hail from non-British backgrounds. It would be unrealistic of us not to accept that that drawing of lines will be the unspoken, and in many cases spoken, backdrop to all which follows. It is, in those circumstances, somewhat unfortunate that the battle lines have already been drawn in a political fashion. Reading some of the speeches on either side would indicate that the Anglo-Irish conflict which has been in existence for hundreds of years will continue to bedevil this debate in Australia. It is no use complaining about it. It is just a fact that we will have to put up with.

The analysis in Dr Saunders' chapter makes it very clear that whatever is done will involve controversial and fundamental changes to our method of government. If the minimalist approach is taken, a whole raft of questions arise, some of which have been touched on in previous chapters and others which will be touched on here. We have already been told that the powers of the Senate, direct election of the Head of State, and the whole issue of responsible government will all have to be considered. Once it is clear that fundamental issues are involved, it is going to be very difficult to avoid all sorts of other important political and social issues coming into the debate. A Bill of Rights will no doubt figure largely, and we will also have a great deal of agitation by people with genuine single interests — Aboriginals, the environment and so on. All will join in the ongoing constitutional debate, and perhaps that is no bad thing. We have already had a thorough examination of constitutional reform through the Constitutional Commission in fairly recent years, and all of those issues will no doubt come back onto the agenda.

Assuming, as I do, that a republic is inevitable, why the concern about it? I will leave aside, for present purposes, those who have an emotional imperative on either side, and concentrate on what I suggest is still a majority of the population who recognise the inevitable cutting of the tie in time, but are concerned about what the consequences may be. What is being lost, what is changing is the identity of the Head of State. What does that involve? It involves little in terms of constitutional theory. The Constitution can, with a little bit of blue pencil and scissors and paste, work tolerably well from a legal point of view if the word "Queen" is removed and the words "Head of State" substituted. However, to do so points to the fundamental issue which would remain, and that is: what type of Head of State would there be? Because presently the powers which reside in the Queen and, through her, the Governor-General, are large indeed. As others have remarked, if one went back to the words of the Constitution, one would not necessarily recognise responsible government as it is practised in Australia today.

An advantage which the ordinary person would perceive at the present time in our political system is that the Head of State, whether it be the Queen or her representative as such, is seen to be above politics. On the other hand, many also believe that the present arrangements constitute a check and balance on the excessive use of power by politicians. It is a little hard to see in theory how that happens if all of the conventions we hear so much about truly exist. But we should be concentrating attention upon these checks and balances. If the Head of State is to be a figurehead, which I think many of us would instinctively like because he or she would not be part of the political process, that would mean that the checks and balances which the present arrangements involve would go. We have a choice to make here. There is a compromise to be made, and I do not think that that has been fully appreciated by people involved in the debate so far.

Most people at the present time believe that if the Governor-General misbehaved very badly he would be removed by the Queen. Some believe that would happen only at the behest of the government of the day, but many others believe that it is, as it were, a reserve power given to the Queen.

Once you remove the foreign Head of State leaving only the local Head of State, that reserve power is removed from the equation and the tenure of the local Head of State becomes critical, particularly if he or she is to have reserve power to dismiss the executive government in certain eventualities. That is not to say that we should not have a local Head of State, rather it is to draw attention to the fact that the present safety net would no longer be there. It appears from reading the accounts of 1975 that both the then Prime Minister and the then Governor-General took the view that the Queen might have removed the Governor-General in mid term at the request of the Prime Minister. That seemed to me then, and still seems to me now, to be a rather odd notion. But it certainly had its very powerful effect both upon what was done and, from reading Sir John Kerr's book,[1] the manner of the doing. So that safety net would be lost with the Crown, and the power of the executive government would, to that extent, be increased. The Head of State may become the pawn of the Prime Minister, unless tenure is dealt with in some other way.

The issues which are addressed here are fundamental because, under our present Constitution, the Crown has two very significant functions, both of which have been touched upon by other contributors to this book.

The first is that the Crown is literally part of the legislature, part of the law-making function. Some of its powers are procedural. Dr Saunders has mentioned several of those — the power of calling, proroguing, dismissing parliament and so on. However, there is a much more direct power, and that is the power of assent, which is constituted by ss 58-60 of the Constitution. Undoubtedly, once the present regime is ended and, with it, the restraints which have so far been implied, it will be necessary to deal with the real effect of ss 58-60. Do we wish the Head of State to be part of the legislature in the present way, and should we have a continuing necessity for assent at all?

The second vital feature of the role of the present Head of State is that the executive power of the Commonwealth is vested in the Queen through the Governor-General, who holds office at her pleasure; and through the Governor-General, in Ministers of State who hold office at the Governor-General's pleasure. The executive role includes Commandership in Chief of the armed forces. It includes the common law prerogative powers of the Crown. It includes the powers given by s 70 of the Constitution. There is no mention of responsible government in the Constitution. The factor which brings it in is the necessity for Ministers of State to be Members of Parliament. Otherwise, you could simply have an American system, with executive power exercised through Ministers of State who do not have to be Members of Parliament, with the executive/legislature relationship governed by the ability to make laws and the ability, in the end, to tax and thus produce supply. Our Constitution does not take that model, it uses the model of the separation of powers, but with the Ministers of State all coming from parliament. There is no particular reason why a Head of State under those circumstances could not take a much more pro-active role in the formation of a government, as do the Presidents or the Heads of State in other places. The necessity that the Ministers of State be

Members of Parliament would be no barrier to a quite different way of organising our affairs than exists at the present time.

If we are to lose the present external Head of State, then I am not sure that British traditions are necessarily the sole answer to our needs. Britain is not a federation, and Britain knows no formal doctrine of the separation of powers. The checks and balances are quite different where you have a hereditary House of Lords to the system which applies with an Australian Senate. I cannot but agree with the comment of Mahoney J (pp 79-80) that one of the big issues that this country is going to face in the next century is the question of the control of executive power, particularly where it is combined with unlimited legislative power. Once we depart from our present arrangements, we will have to consider very carefully the method of achieving the checks and balances which so far, by and large, have proved unnecessary, and so effective.

It is fundamental to understand that what we are dealing with here is the tension between the executive and the legislature. There is also the greater potential involvement of the judiciary in political issues. Once you start to write down conventions, you must have consensus as to what they are and they immediately become justiciable. I do not favour the view that the judges should play a large part in law-making. I think they administer the law well but do not necessarily make the law well. More importantly, the greater the quasi-political role the judiciary plays, the greater the risk of undermining public confidence in its impartiality, with all that involves for law and order in society.

COMMENTARY

ENTRENCHING BRITISH VALUES IN THE CONSTITUTION

Justice Bannon (NSW Land & Environment Court)

Regarding Roger Gyles' reference to the Irish, I have a number of Irish ancestors, some of whom lost their heads at the behest of the British monarchy. But the Crown in Australia represents the underlying morals, sources of law and ethics in our community. Sir Owen Dixon pointed out[1] that our Commonwealth has a common law and while all the republicans want to get rid of the Crown, they also want to get rid of the Union Jack, which represents England, Ireland and Scotland, and they say Australia has suddenly become a multicultural nation, something our Constitution does not mention. I think that if we are going to have a change, it is at least necessary to write into our Constitution some reference to the underlying morals, and common law and ethics which have guided British peoples in the past and which I hope will still continue to guide Australia in the future. If we do not do that, we will end up in the same multicultural confusion as the United States.

Roger Gyles

Each of us will be impressed or not impressed by arguments about multiculturalism so far as the republican debate is concerned. It is of no particular interest to me what people from non-English-speaking backgrounds might think about it. They have a perfect right to their view, and if they present a powerful intellectual argument, then I will agree with it. If they are in sufficient numbers to carry the vote on the day, then I will go along with their decision. However, I do not feel I have any duty in conscience to not follow my particular point of view about this matter in deference to others, any more than I am in the slightest concerned what people in other countries, whether they be in Asia or Europe, think about our link with the Crown. But, having said that, I must say that if the Constitution as it evolves does properly reflect our political process, then it seems to me we must trust that process to arrive at a result which the majority of the population will accept. One assumes that because of our history and our political background we will continue to have a strong basis in the Anglo-Saxon tradition, but I do not think entrenching it in the Constitution has any long-term future.

COMPULSORY VOTING AND FIXED TERMS

Q   (to Cheryl Saunders)

What are your views on compulsory voting and fixed terms?

Cheryl Saunders

We are one of the few countries in the world that does have compulsory voting. People on both sides of the debate claim democratic virtue for their points. The polls tend to show that so far quite a substantial majority of Australians support compulsory voting apparently on the grounds that it is more fair. It may be. It may be that it is part of a very democratic culture in Australia, of which the fact that we vote to change our Constitution is another part. But I think that compulsory voting is something upon which decent people may reasonably differ, and I am sure that debate will be back again and again.

On the subject of fixed terms, there are parliaments all over Australia introducing fixed terms or partially fixed terms. Victoria has three-year fixed terms subject to exceptions; New South Wales has a fixed term for the current parliament;. Tasmania has just introduced a fixed term for its current parliament; South Australia has a partially fixed term. So fixed terms are being experimented with here at present and it is certain that if we move to a discussion of four-year terms for the House of Representatives, fixed terms will be back on the political agenda.

CHOOSING A HEAD OF STATE

Q

Some thought needs to be given to the term of office of a Head of State, whether for a fixed term, whether the term would be renewable or whether for life. Is the possibility of an hereditary Head of State to be considered, or is the idea totally repugnant? If it is not totally repugnant, what might we call such a Head of State?

Cheryl Saunders

As far as the term is concerned, I certainly think it should be fixed, and it should be for a longer period than the life of a current government, so probably it should be a five-year or a seven-year term. The longer it gets, the greater the argument for having it non-renewable, and on balance I would prefer a longer one that is non-renewable. These are all matters for argument. Personally, I would not make it for life or hereditary. Think of all the problems we would have of identifying the lucky family.

Roger Gyles

I would add that it is very much bound up with who does the appointing. If it is an executive appointment, then there is a very strong case for a long term, that is, a term extending beyond a parliamentary term. If it is to be a parliamentary appointment, perhaps similar considerations apply. If it were direct election, then perhaps one would have a different view about it. Removal would similarly be a most vital question. I have assumed that a term would be fixed, save for specified grounds for removal.

Kim Santow

On the question of dismissal of the Head of State, with the Kerr-Whitlam dismissal, one of the issues was the so-called race to the

Queen, with a Head of State needing to dismiss a government in order to prevent the government getting in first and dismissing the Head of State. In the Saunders minimalist model, though as much power as possible is taken away from the Head of State in order to make the Constitution self-executing, yet some of the reserve powers to dismiss the government may actually be left. We can assume the government would in turn have the power to dismiss the Head of State. This could be on any ground, such as proven misbehaviour or simply at pleasure. What if, having dismissed the Head of State, or simply failed to appoint a new one, the Head of State's fixed term having expired, there is *no* Head of State to intervene in a Constitutional crisis? Possibly the crisis may have actuated this dismissal? Under the present system such a lacuna is not possible as the Queen can ensure there is not.

Cheryl Saunders

Whatever model is adopted for power, some provision for removal is necessary. Even if it was purely a figurehead role, it is possible that someone could simply go crazy and would need to be removed from office. It never seemed to me that in 1975 the race to the palace had much reality behind it, although I could see that the players probably thought that it did. My own view is that the Queen would have accepted advice to remove Sir John Kerr eventually, but she was hardly going to be answering the phone in the palace at three o'clock in the morning. And she was very unlikely to dismiss on advice that was given over the phone anyway. So there would have been considerable delay, and by that stage the events would have played themselves out here. That is another advantage of the present system. The delay creates a hiccup between decisions and actions. Again, the method that could be adopted for removing a Head of State would depend a bit on the method that is adopted for putting them there in the first place. I would favour having the Constitution prescribe the grounds for removal much in the same way as it is done for judges. I do not think that there should be additional grounds. If there were, for example, to be a system whereby a special majority of the parliament appoint the Head of State, it would be appropriate to have a similar process for removal. And whether there would be some fact-finding process first, or whether it would simply be left to the political process, is another question. If there were a popularly elected Head of State, the method of removal would obviously be rather more difficult. What the Irish constitution does about that may be of significance.

Roger Gyles

In principle, there is a real argument for having no grounds for dismissal at all, save for infirmity. Once dismissal is based in any way upon conduct, the opportunities for mischief are very great.

Q

Both sides of the argument say that the almost universal aspiration of us all is to have a Head of State who is above politics. Yet even when beginning to address the question of choosing a Head of State, every possible method that is put forward ends up being a political decision. How can that be done except through hereditary means?

Cheryl Saunders

The problem is that we do not really have a Head of State now who is above politics. Certainly the Queen's position is hereditary and she is the formal Head of State. The relationship between the Queen and the Governor-General, and the role that the Governor-General now plays in Australia have evolved to such an extent that really the Governor-General is the de facto Head of State. While that appointment is filtered through the prism of the Crown, it is essentially a political appointment — a much more political appointment than any of the methods that are canvassed in this book, because it is an appointment by the government of the day. And it has been that way since 1930. I agree with you that it is very hard to work out a system which will remove politics from the appointment. Therefore we need to focus not just on the technical method of appointment, which I think is important, but also on the precedents that we established very early on. If we can establish precedents of appointing a few terrific Heads of State, whether they are called bunyips or presidents, that will stand us in good stead for the future.

COMMENTARY

Q

The Presidency in Ireland is an unusual one. It has virtually no powers. The present incumbent of the office is a very talented, and from this distance, very successful President, Mary Robinson. Would that be a good analogy from our point of view and perhaps would that be an answer to the problem — is she in fact seen as above politics in Ireland?

Cheryl Saunders

Mary Robinson has been a wonderful President for Ireland. I gather that most of the previous incumbents of the office have not been quite so wonderful, however, and that there has been a tendency for the major political parties to put up someone who is sometimes a bit of a hack, and for the political process to take a course that we would be rather more familiar with. Mary Robinson was in fact a candidate for a minor party when she became President but slipped through the middle, when one of the parties fell off the tram, or maybe the galloping train, at some stage. But it is also true that there is very little actual formal power in the Irish presidency. One power that does exist, which nobody discusses here because we do not happen to have it at present — that is the power to refer unconstitutional bills to the Supreme Court to get an opinion on their validity before they come into force. But, apart from that, the power is very limited and I gather that she is very closely watched by her advisers.

SUMMING UP

Kim Santow

Professor Lang Wu in his 1992 Bonython lecture to the Centre for Independent Studies summed up Australia rather aptly. He said we were a middle-ranking power. Our value in Asia was as a trusted intermediary between Europe and the United States on the one hand and Asia on the other. That we were able to participate more readily because we were free of the incubus of a colonial past. How does that relate to the decision to be a republic? Superficially, one might say that to become a republic will make us more attractive to Asia, but I think that is nonsense, at least in that superficial sense. What is significant though, is the way in which we do it, the tone in which we do it, and perhaps the symbolism of what we are doing. After all, if our role is to be an intermediary, then perhaps our role should be an intermediary with the Europe that the United Kingdom has embraced and not just an intermediary with the United Kingdom. One important aspect of that decision of becoming a republic will be to say that our relationship remains close to the United Kingdom, but it is not exclusive to the United Kingdom, just as the United Kingdom made its own choice when it embraced Europe. I think it also symbolises that APEC is not a mere trading block, but an outward looking group of nations in this region. And if we can keep a foot in both camps, if we are not ashamed of our British links, but rather state that we have broader links than that, outside our region as well as within, then perhaps republicanism will serve us well. It will also make us closer to the Commonwealth, which, after all, is a predominantly Asian grouping.

The Constitution should so far as possible not place the Head of State under the intolerable strain of dismissing a government, except perhaps in the very limited sense of determining after an election whether there is a government in place which commands the support of the lower house. If we end up with a Constitution which effectively removes the need for reserve powers, then I think a lot of the difficulties of the move to a republic will be diminished. While legal matters may have an archaic feel about them, the Constitution is a matter that rightly affects us all. Cheryl Saunders observed that the process whereby we reach a consensus to become a republic, if indeed that is the outcome, will be a maturing process and a binding process. And in that very process, may do more to establish a real and evolving sense of national identity than anything else.

One of the difficulties Cheryl Saunders' model still leaves us grappling with is the fact that when the process is self-executing, the capacity for an independent person outside the political process to advise and warn, and in that process to try to produce an outcome that is achieved consensually rather than by use of those reserve powers, is to some extent removed. However, if the reserve powers

COMMENTARY

are not there, then the advice and consent may have a greater degree of trust and confidence attached to it.

V

IDENTIFYING WITH ASIA

INTRODUCTION

Pamela Gutman

It has often been alleged that the fact of Australia becoming a republic was not of particular importance to the countries of our region. I do not agree.

In 1972 when I was in Burma, Prime Minister Gough Whitlam made an announcement distancing Australia from the monarchy. It was perceived by my Burmese colleagues that Australia was becoming a republic, and the idea was roundly congratulated. Recently, a number of articles have appeared in the Indonesian media about the republican debate, and the response has, for Republicans, been immensely encouraging, with particular interest in the possibility of Australia leaving its colonial history behind and now becoming "one of us". In this context we should mention that Australia's role in the Indonesian independence movement is still remembered there, and is one of the important parts of our relationship. As has been pointed out, countries in our region are in the process of redefining themselves, with a number of different factors bearing on this redefinition, not least economic factors.

Australia, together with Japan and the countries of Western Europe, is now entering into a post-industrialised phase of history. However, North-East Asians, apart from Japan, and the countries of ASEAN (the Association of South-East Asian Nations) are industrialising. Their economies are growing fairly rapidly in many cases, causing very dynamic changes in their respective societies. One of these changes, arguably the most important, is the growth of the middle classes. We are constantly being told in the financial media that this growth is particularly important for Australia because the middle classes are potential consumers of Australian products and services. But the question goes much wider than that. The middle classes are moving away from the traditional elite domination of their societies. Middle-class Chinese overseas are becoming particularly important in their roles as entrepreneurs.

Alongside this, Australia and the Asian countries are experiencing the impact of cultural globalisation brought about by the internationalisation of the world economy, the emergence of truly multinational companies and the impact of the electronic media. For instance, we now have Asian acceptance of international designer brands such as Louis Vuitton and Gucci, because many of these countries are not yet very sure of their own cultural redefinition and are choosing such internationally accepted models.

Alison Broinowski, the author of *The Yellow Lady*[1] is now Director of Advocacy and Planning in the Australia Council, and was formerly an officer of the Department of Foreign Affairs and Trade. Her chapter is concerned with what she perceives to be the problems Australia has in finding its own regional identity, and compares this with the continuing redefinition of Japanese and other cultures. She then turns to the possible role of an Australia Foundation.

The Australian intellectual tradition related to Asia is a very important one. There has been a long tradition of Oriental Studies or Asian Studies in Australia. Our scholars are internationally recognised now as being at the forefront of explaining Asia to the rest of the world and to Asia itself. We are perhaps the only country in the region where Asia can learn about itself in a relatively neutral manner. Our economists have done important work towards the liberalisation of the world economy and their advice is sought in regional matters. Historians and other academics have great status in the region's think tanks. One such academic is Tony Milner, who himself belongs to one of Australia's best-known think tanks, the Academy of Social Sciences at the Australian National University.

Dr Milner is Reader in History at the Australian National University and Director of the Australian Academy of Social Sciences' research project on Australian Asian Perceptions. A specialist on South-East Asia, he has written widely on Malay history. His most recent book, a study of the ideological conflicts in Malaysia, "The Invention of Politics", is to be published early next year by Cambridge University Press.

An Australian Presence in Asia?
An Australia Foundation?

Alison Broinowski

This chapter will address the question of why it is that images are important, with the proposition that Australia has image problems, suggesting what they are and how they might be addressed.

Few would deny that Japan has had an image problem in its recent history, a serious one stemming from World War II. Some Australians refuse to let that die — Australians who, curiously enough, do not mind too much about Vietnam, but who nevertheless insist on still treating Japan as a perennial enemy. Curiously such attitudes to Vietnam and Japan are reversed in the United States.

Japan, of course, is aware of its image problem. It has become a prosperous country and has poured money into redeeming itself in international and national esteem. It has done this by a process not only of image cultivation, through such organisations as the Japan Foundation, but also by a process of waiting, watching and keeping a low profile.

Australia has, I believe, an image problem differing in origins but similar in dimension to that of Japan. But we have not acknowledged it nor have we devoted to it the sorts of resources, the sort of waiting and watching time the Japanese have had the good sense to do.

Our image problem derives from three things. The first is the White Australia Policy. From 1968 to 1975 the White Australia Policy was progressively dismantled, but although it was declared dead and buried in 1973, the burial required more and more heaping on of sods and saying of last rites before Australians themselves could be convinced that it was gone. News of this burial process did not speedily reach our neighbours, nor indeed any other country in the world, so that the idea of the White Australia Policy is still rooted currently in many of the countries where I have lived and among many of the peoples with whom I have worked.

Partly this is because we have not got that message out clearly or convincingly enough, and partly, because every now and again, even among the people we may have already convinced, various individual Australians regress, giving resounding declarations that it is still alive and well. In 1988 for instance, the statements made by John Howard, Leader of the Federal Opposition, about Asian immigration, and repeated since, were reported on the front page of Hong Kong newspapers. This only served to convince people that Australians had, in fact, not changed their attitudes or policies. The unspoken belief remains that with a change of government or a change of political emphasis, these views will revive.

Of course Australia is not alone in having had a restrictive immigration policy — almost every country in the world has had restrictive immigration of one kind or another, and in many countries that restrictiveness is racial. America and Canada both had the equivalent of a White Australia Policy, although they did not call it that and they did not go around the world trumpeting it. By giving the policy a slogan name that was readily repeated in newspaper headlines, it has stuck in peoples' memories. The White Australia policy is still recorded as current in textbooks in many Asian countries. Whatever we may think about ourselves, and even if it is not accurate, children in schools in some Asian countries are still being taught about the White Australia Policy as if it were still in operation.

The second cause of our image problem is Australian ignorance about Asian countries, an ignorance which, together with arrogance, is the worst possible combination of attitudes to have about the region. As I tried to show in *The Yellow Lady*,[1] many people still adhere to images of Asia which have been long out of date, as out of date as their image of us as a restrictive immigration country.

Among those images which occur frequently is the idea that all of Asia is a monolith, and the assumption that one can actually talk about Asia as a whole. A positive or a negative image is generalised to include the whole region, depending upon one's point of view. A positive image of Asia emphasises its traditions, artistry, philosophies and exoticism, or its modern technological and economic achievements. In the negative image, Asia is seen as overcrowded, unsanitary and dangerous, with a low standard of living, poor human rights, dictatorships, various forms of religious and ethnic barbarity and corruption.

Very often such sentiments are accompanied by the question what do they, the Asians, think of us? That question is absolutely unanswerable, because one has to ask who "they" means, that is, which of the two-thirds of the world's population. If the reply is "the Chinese", which of those 1.3 billion people? Then we narrow it down again and again until a particular answer is elicited, like Prime Minister Mahathir, who is not Chinese but Malaysian. South-East Asia is often equated by Australians with all of Asia. The geographical myopia that still afflicts some Australians is a hangover of the eurocentric education system with which they grew up.

The third factor underlying our image problem is ignorance or arrogance about Australia on the part of Asians in the region. The causes of this have several sources, including xenophobia and prejudice, which are not confined to us Australians. We have to address the ignorance, but there is not a lot we can do about the arrogance. It is all very well for us to say that people in the region should inform themselves better about Australia — perhaps they should. But we are the newcomers, the ones who came into the region and set up shop here. We are the ones whose forebears arrived but did not visit our neighbouring countries to inquire about how to cope with typhoons, or how to develop tropical agriculture, or about herbal remedies for malaria and green bamboo snake bite. Instead, our forebears came to this part of the world with an attitude of superior wisdom — of being here to teach and instruct, with the original attitude I mentioned earlier of arrogance combined with ignorance.

Clearly we have wasted 200 years. For decades our education system was devoid of Asian content, apart from a few centres like Sydney University, which set up a Department of Oriental Studies in 1918 and which was exceptional in its day. Until the current generation, Asian content was marginalised in our education system. Asian history, literature and philosophy were taught as Asian Studies, not as part of the major disciplines. I had no opportunity at my university to be taught about Asia. I had to educate myself about it as an adult. Fortunately, this is the last generation in which that will be the case. But we have wasted time and there is a lot of catching up to do. Only when we have done so will we have some grounds for suggesting to our neighbours in the region that we do know about them, and that we are trying to renegotiate their images of us.

Another source of problems affecting our image in the region is self-generated. Although there are now Australian Studies courses in universities, and more contact between universities in Australia and those in the Asia region, some Australians have a residual tendency to put their own country down in Asian countries. Some of the worst sinners in this regard are Australian business people, because for whatever reason, political or economic, they consistently "bad mouth" Australia. The impression that leaves on the people they are talking to is unlikely to be favourable or to give them the idea that Australia is a worthwhile place in which to do business. Although we are accustomed to being self-critical within Australia, such self-criticism does not impress anybody in the neighbouring region. The self-flagellation and lack of self-worth that used to be called the cultural cringe has not yet gone away.

In its newest manifestation, this cringing behaviour is interpreted by countries in the region as "Australians are poor business people, they're untrustworthy". In the minds of some, the Australian business failures of the 1980s and the early 1990s prove the point. Countries like Japan and Korea, which within living memory were both comprehensively flattened, and Singapore, which started from nothing, had nothing but their belief in themselves with which to get going. They did not have the natural resources that Australians take for granted. Belief in ourselves is what Australia lacks. We have all the advantages, but we still do not clearly know who we are, nor how to advance that in our own interests.

Finally, another source of this poor reputation of ours is that our own media make self-critical statements of a kind which would not be permitted in some regional countries, but which are readily picked up and put on the front pages of major Asian newspapers. The more critical we are of ourselves in the media, the more those stories are reported in the region, adding to our poor reputation.

There is little we can do about that unless we are going to condone censorship. However, I think we do need to see if we can produce more success stories, as indeed the government is trying to do, on trade and on our pluralist society, and promote those attributes to other countries in the region.

On a more positive note, some exciting things are happening in education and in trade. For example, Monash University has established a consultancy program in China on Higher Education, is setting up a university in Saigon, and has a contract from the Vietnamese Government to take all Vietnamese Government-sponsored students. Another example is the Sydney University campus which has been established in Penang, Malaysia, where students study for two or three years, qualifying for entry into any major university in New South Wales.

Sixty percent of Australia's trade is with Asia; our trade with South-East Asia is growing more rapidly than trade with any other region; and the trade with ASEAN countries is greater than our trade with the United States. In fact Australia is the third largest economy in the Asia Pacific region.

It is worth remembering that over 40 percent of our migrants are from Asian countries. Australia, since 1945, has taken in 4.5 million people from 130 different cultures — a source of some pride, and a fact we ought to be projecting into the region to displace the images that are still current.

Yet a sense of estrangement from Asia and an emphasis on difference persist in Australian minds. There are two ways to get over this. One is to work on all fronts towards accepting Asia as part of the Australian main-stream, without question and in every forum and activity and the other is to improve our image.

In everything we do we should seek to be linked with the Asian region: in sporting associations, in trade organisations, in professional bodies and so on, rather than seeking always to be associated with countries on the other side of the world. If we do this in every field of our activity, we acquire a better knowledge of the strong and weak points of our neighbourhood. The national interest is vitally affected by the way Australia is seen in the region. Whatever rational arguments may be advanced, it is whether the image of Australia is a respectable, reliable and impressive country, or a self-doubting, ineffective country, that is going to make the difference to what decisions are made.

It is our responsibility to do work on improving our image, and it is vitally important to Australia that we do so. We have become a big education provider and that helps. However, it is very difficult to buy a recently published Australian book in most Asian countries. Australian publishers do not promote, export, nor try hard enough to sell in those Asian countries where we are trying to create and change our image. If an Australian wants to produce an Australian film, he or she usually goes to Cannes or Los Angeles to do it; and a multinational film distributor may then decide to promote it in the Asian region. We must penetrate the markets of importance to us, or we will remain subject to the colonial forms of cultural distribution which persist in the English-speaking world.

The Australian Government has been working for years on image creation and has spent millions and millions of dollars over a very long time. It is like dropping pennies down a well. Thousands of Australian exhibitions, performances, displays, promotions and individuals have been sent into the neighbouring region but it is still not enough, because our overall image is still deficient.

In my opinion the time has come for what I call an "Australia Foundation" — a sort of a replica of the British Council but more like the Japan Foundation, whose task is to improve Japan's image abroad. An Australia Foundation differs from the Australia Council in that while the Foundation might promote the arts, it could not do so as a patron, but only as a means of improving the national image.

There are three ways this can be done. First by using the arts, in the very broadest sense, including even sport and science; second, by using education inside and outside Australia; and third by using information programs. We have the tools to do this in government already, and thus these goals should be able to be achieved in almost a cost-neutral way. This is important because we have previously been held back by insufficient government funds. Such a Foundation (not to be confused with the proposed Foundation for Australian Cultural Development) could use the stepping stones which are already in place in the cultural area of Foreign Affairs and Trade, at the moment managed by the Australia Abroad Council. The education side could evolve by basing it on the system of Australian Education Centres established in several Asian countries by the International Development Program of Australian universities and colleges. The information area could come from the Overseas Information Branch of the Department of Foreign Affairs and Trade. Each organisation would lose something, each would also benefit. The Foundation could operate in association with Australian Embassies abroad, so there would be an office of the Australia Foundation in many countries where there is an Australian Embassy. By following the Japan Foundation model, the size and scope of the office depends upon the importance of the country and the problems facing us with the national image in each country. Thus, in a place where Australia's image is assessed to be reasonably satisfactory, we would not put in as much effort as, perhaps, to a country where we have a real problem. While there are people in government working on this idea now, it must be stressed such a Foundation has as yet no official status at all.

The idea is but one response to dealing with our image problem, albeit an important one at this time of renegotiation of Australia's identity, the re-interpretation of our place in the region, and our role in the world. It can be argued that we have a greater problem with regard to national image than any other country. What does Australia export? Raw materials and primary products, and little which shows it is made in Australia. We lack a classy image of consumer products such as those made in France or Italy, and this is partly why we have to work harder than most other countries. We must project a positive image of ourselves; nobody else is going to do it for us.

Australian-Asian Perceptions

Anthony Milner

The Australian-Asian Perceptions Project, of which I am Director, is highly relevant to the possible operations of the "Australia Foundation" discussed by Alison Broinowski, and indeed to the whole issue of Australian identity. The Academy of the Social Sciences in Australia, in fact, anticipated much of the current discussion when it proposed the project to the Australian Research Council. The Academy noted that reports had already been written on Australia's strategic and economic position in Asia and decided that it was time to look at the cultural underpinnings of Australia's relations in the region.

Differences in culture or world view, of course, can cause misunderstanding and confusion in relations between nations and peoples. The Academy Project has looked at specific issues relating to trade, human rights, the media, national security and many other areas critical to Australia's regional involvements.

At another level, the project tackles the question of this country's "otherness", what Foreign Minister Gareth Evans has called "our unique character and position as seen by our neighbours". It is this second level of study which makes a particular contribution to discussion on cultural identity and change, and to determining the sort of policy and direction that a body such as an Australia Foundation might follow.

The Australian-Asian Perceptions Project has been concerned on the one hand with case studies in Australian-Asian relations, and on the other with comparative studies which look at the way our perceptions differ from those operating in specific Asian societies — perceptions in areas such as labour relations, business ethics, national security, the education process, human rights and democracy.

We organised a series of "composition meetings" or workshops, lasting about five days each and involving six to nine people from different disciplines who were specialists on different countries in the region. Some of these specialists were from the region itself. The Department of Foreign Affairs and Trade, the Department of Defence, Austrade and various universities helped us to bring people to Australia for these sessions. In each session we had an "Australianist", and this was an important feature of the process. It is very rare, as many academics know, to bring specialists on Australia together with specialists on Asian countries.

During composition meetings the different writing groups prepared research papers, but only after exhaustive discussions. In considering contrasting perceptions or cultural difference, we took the view that culture was not a static thing. Cultures are constantly changing, being re-shaped and reconstructed; they are even invented, sometimes deliberately and sometimes by accident. In a single society there are often competing cultures, and in certain cases competing perceptions of one culture.

In the composition meetings, the Australianists played a particularly important role. They reacted to the Asian specialists, often reformulating their own views of Australia in an Asian context.

In the comparisons we made between Australian and Asian societies, certain common elements were immediately evident. One element, obvious enough, concerned government. A particularly distinguished American specialist on early South-East Asian societies and government presented an account of what government was like in the pre-colonial period of Asian history. This account, which drew attention to the exoticism of early Asian political forms, underscored how very similar our approaches are to government today in both

Australian and Asian societies. When we compare the pre-colonial view — in which "government" tends to be understood frequently in terms of its ceremonial, religious, cosmological or didactic functions — with the current situation, there appears to be much in common between the political forms which prevail in Australia and most Asian states. All the governments in the region today are "active" governments. Their legitimacy is presented in terms of their contribution to development policies: it is performance legitimacy. They are "to do" governments rather than "to be" governments (to use a distinction elaborated in a well-known textbook on South-East Asia) and act in a developmental, improving way.

A further common element in most Asian countries and Australia today — something too seldom reflected upon — is the presence of some form of "public sphere", some notion of "the people" as a body to which those who govern are responsible. A Vietnam specialist, Greg Lockhart (originally from Sydney University) pinpointed this development in the case of Vietnam to about 1900. He cited an instance when a Vietnamese thinker used the phrase "the country of Vietnam has people". This was considered to be an extraordinarily revolutionary statement at the time. It entailed a focus on the people rather than on the King, a shift which may not amount to the introduction of a full-scale democracy but does infer that the government must at the very least address the people, and govern on behalf of the people.

Other common elements in numerous areas which we investigated were identified and discussed. Each country in the region, including Australia, has labour relations problems; moreover there is widespread respect for democracy, citizenship and human rights (and these terms are used all over the region, even though they often have different meanings or significations in different places).

It is the distinctive Australian characteristics, however, which matter for the purpose of this book. When the Academy Project considered the issue of citizenship, for instance, we examined what the concept of citizenship means in different countries within the region, noting a number of striking aspects in the Australian situation.

It is easier in Australia to get citizenship, of course, at least once you're here, than it is in most countries in the region. Yet we seldom spell out what citizenship means to us. The term itself seems to have some emotive power, at least used in a negative way: "second class citizenship" is a strong statement in Australia, and the way Malaysia, for instance, seems to treat some of its citizens differently from others is viewed as repugnant by many ordinary Australians. These Australians do not know the very convincing reasons why Malaysians of "Malay" ethnic identification have been given certain privileges. The fact that Australians do not tend to make explicit their positive notions of citizenship is especially confusing for immigrants to this country.[1] The Academy writing group found this to be the case in its discussions with Asian community leaders in Perth. The leaders also expressed surprise at the lack in Australia of a strong sense of national loyalty or patriotism associated with citizenship.

When we compared Australia with most Asian societies, even those which had experienced European political and constitutional ideas, we found that it is the communitarian rather than the individualistic dimension of citizenship that predominated in the latter. When the 19th and 20th century ideologues in Asian countries encountered Western thought, they took those aspects which seemed to serve their own long-standing interests, chiefly those stressing the commitment of the subject to the community. The words used for "citizen" in certain Asian countries, for instance, convey a sense of citizenship as membership of a family or of a royal community. In their perception of citizenship there is a special emphasis on community, and on the subject's duties to the community rather than the rights of the individual subject. By contrast, in Australia, the notion of citizenship contains much of the sort of inherited European tradition of rights as well as responsibilities of the individual citizen. It sees the citizen as an individual actor in the polity, and this tradition goes back, of course, to the classical period, to 15th century Italy, and to 17th and 18th century England and the United States.

Finally, when we reflect on citizenship in Australia, it is clear that the term today is remarkably free of any ethnic connotation. Again this perception is in direct contrast with that prevailing in many Asian societies. In Japan, Korea and numerous other Asian societies, the link between citizenship and ethnicity is extremely strong. In certain countries — as already noted — different ethnicities determine different classes or levels of citizenship. The current contrast between these countries and Australia can be described provocatively. One might argue that in the White Australia Policy days we were, at least in one sense, perhaps more "Asian" than we are today.

Another Academy Project session considered perceptions and expectations of government. An important distinction was made between the strength of government and the intrusiveness of government. Australia's strong democratic traditions and its federal system limits the strength of government in society in this country, yet by many Asian standards our government is intrusive in its scope. Compared with numerous countries, Australia does not have a particularly strong government in terms of long-term, effective planning. But our government is intrusive in the way it mediates in many areas such as unemployment, health, child abuse and gender relations. Australians expect government to intervene in such areas. We are comfortable with random breath testing; we are critical of government when somebody falls off a cliff, and ask why the authorities did not place a protective fence there. We take a relatively positive attitude to government. It is different, for instance, from that of some Cambodian immigrants to this country who, having lost their jobs, and been told that the government will provide training schemes for them, declare that to be involved with government is the last thing on earth they want. They have a very negative view of government, a fear of government that is generally rare in Australian society.

In one sphere, however, we Australians are very wary of government action. We are less comfortable than many Asian societies with the government assuming a strong and overt ideological role. We are cautious about the sort of role government plays in Indonesia when it inculcates the *panca sila* ideology in Indonesian society. The Malaysian Government's propagation of its *ruku negara* ideology, or similar action by Chinese and Vietnamese Governments, also arouse suspicion.

The Australian Government, too, has ideological concerns — multiculturalism is one of them — but they are advocated in a much less explicit fashion. And even as the citizens of Australia call upon government to give ideological guidance in specific areas — for instance in matters relating to the environment or to gender relations — the broad notion of government as teacher or maker of ideology is less acceptable in Australian than in most Asian societies. Australian Government may be intrusive but we do not like it to be blatantly so — indeed, it would probably surprise and disturb many Australians to be pressed to reflect upon just how far we have gone in accepting intrusive government in this country.

In considering the scope of government, Australians are more comfortable with formulations that stress the government's duty to satisfy the rights and freedoms of its citizens as individuals. This is the way government interventions in society must be justified.

The primacy of the individual, of individualism, is also central when we consider human rights. And this is indeed a further topic which was examined in a Project workshop. It was in the "human rights" session that the Asian participants were most explicit and also pungent in their comments. They distrusted Australia's preoccupation with human rights. They wondered about our motives. People who have read about the recent debates on human rights issues in Asia know of the contest of views, and of the suggestion in certain quarters that Western human rights diplomacy is some sort of hangover or substitute for colonialism.

Australia's own human rights preoccupations are sometimes seen in this light, and partly also as an expression of the anxiety of an isolated Western country which is anxious to obtain international assistance in making its Asian neighbours less potentially threatening. Certainly, our human rights concerns are remarkably Western and liberal. They show little concern, for instance, for Islamic rights and other non-Western rights. They are also Western and liberal in that they give so much stress to *individual* rather than *group* rights. In fact, one of the most eloquent contributors to our session on human rights — a Singaporean — demonstrated that the type of defence of group rights argued by his own Singapore Government, attracts a good deal of sincere support in the actual population of the State. The Singapore Government's perception of the West, he told us, is that it is intoxicated with individualism, and that this hedonistic self-serving individualism justifies, first, an endless list of citizens' claims on the State and, secondly, an unwillingness on the part of Western governments to push aside narrow individual rights on behalf of the far more significant broader community welfare. Examples of the latter are found in such areas as national security and public housing.

To approach the issue of human rights from the other perspective — that is, the perspective commonly expressed in Australia — the preoccupation with the individual leads Australians to misjudge or recode apparent human rights transgressions. As one participant expressed it, in many situations Australians create human rights situations by their own definitions.

A further Australian perception or value which clouds our vision in human rights cases arises from the adversarial system which prevails in our legal tradition. Because of this tradition, we are disturbed by the idea that confession is considered as the basis of conviction in China and Japan. In an inquisitorial system, which some countries possess, where the judge has the duty to investigate rather than merely adjudicate, confession may be understood in different terms. But our starting point in Australia is the adversarial system.

The adversarial approach, it might be added, is influential also in other spheres — in labour relations, for instance. Although our composition meeting on this topic came to the conclusion that tension in the work place existed in all countries in the region, the actual style of labour relations in Australia is certainly adversarial. In many Asian countries more stress is placed on harmony, hierarchy, paternalism and so forth. Where labour difficulties do exist, open conflict is less acceptable than in Australia — though any generalisation must take into account the dramatic conflict which has taken place in Korea.

The point here is a little reminiscent of the observation made in the session on education, where, once again, the stress in Australia is on dialectical engagement. Knowledge is not seen to flow down from teacher to class, rather the teacher is understood to engage dialectically with the individual student. Of course, even at university in Australia, the teacher specifically teaches the student to write a seemingly individualistic, well-argued essay. And one good essay does look remarkably like another good essay. What is significant here is that we perceive the process of learning in different terms. We stress originality, the individual response and so forth. And the Asian student in Australia, as a result, often finds our system non-supportive, lonely and coldly impersonal. Academics seem to them concerned to provoke rather than to guide.

In the discussions which took place in such workshops as those on education, human rights and citizenship, we came to realise the long-reaching implications of individualism.

Another key element in the Western "liberal" package is that of the nation-state, and this element seems to be especially potent in Australian thinking about a further topic, national security. Asian participants in this session commented on Australia's quite vigorous concern for national security and also on the way we stress military security. They thought we were quite preoccupied with security and military matters; in fact, even in the academic sphere, they noted with just a hint of criticism that we have made a greater contribution internationally in this area than in many others. We seem to be good at "military security", they said. It was suggested too that Australians more than most people in the region tend to be comfortable with the "realist" conception of a world of competing nation-states. We think in terms of states and assume they compete with one another. We have a clear sense of Australia as a geographical entity, a nation-state with clearly defined borders, and assume that all the other countries in the region can be classified in just this fashion. Australians are often insensitive, however, to the fact that many Asian countries perceive themselves and the international environment in different terms.

For example, in some societies the ethnic unit is considered to be even more important than a nation-state unit. In other societies there may be a hierarchical view of relations between peoples, and that hierarchical structure may transcend the divisions between nation-states. Do some Chinese leaders, for instance, see the world in terms of civilisation rather than state, with the middle kingdom of China at the centre? In the case of ethnicity, it is hard for us today to appreciate the possibility that maintaining Japanese racial purity is seen as a national security issue in Japan.

It is not possible here to convey the subtleties — and there were many subtleties — arising in the Academy Project's discussions. What can be stressed is that in the case of Australia, what came through persistently in our deliberations set in the Australian-Asian context, is the significance of the liberal ideological package. The nation-state, the individual, the egalitarianism, the democratic decision-making, the adversarial debate tradition are all central. The presence of debate, for instance, is considered to be the sign of a so-called healthy society.

Moving next to the media session, we noted various responsibilities and perceptions of the media in Australia. The often ritualistic way in which news services take pains to present debate was remarked upon. These services may seek no more than two points of view — Labor and the Coalition — and vigorously exclude all other perspectives, but so long as there is not only just one point of view the requirement of debate is considered to have been satisfied.

A very prominent Indonesian participant, at present working in Australia, commented on this from another angle. He argued that our press is irresponsible, lacking in long-term strategies and any sort of national commitment. Our press criticises for criticism's sake. The Indonesian press, he says, has been enmeshed with nationalism for decades; it attempts to contribute to the development of the nation, to criticise government constructively. He said this in the presence of Donald Horne, who articulates so well the significance of the adversarial tradition in making Australia a healthy society.

In the political sphere, when we examine "democracy", a Japanese participant was amazed to watch the broadcast of parliament on television. He saw a Prime Minister and an Opposition Leader — whose policies by the standards of many countries in the region were very similar to one another — engage in vicious debate, standing almost face to face, saliva distance, cutting one another apart before a national audience. At moments like this, with the Japanese participant watching such a scene on television during his first visit to Australia, the Australian participants were indeed able to see Australia as the "other".

We are the "other", with our tradition of debate, freedom and individualism. We can see ourselves as the "other", too, with our stress on equality and on the rights of the citizen. Our abhorrence of hierarchy and of grades of citizenship, and our discomfort with the notion of an ideology-imposing government or the idea of a too-vigorous official nationalism are also distinctive Australian features in an Asian context.

A good deal has been said in this volume about common values in Australia — and yet, few of these values tend to be identified. The Academy Project suggests that when Australia is examined in the Asian context, we have an opportunity to make explicit some of the key values and concepts which operate in Australian society. When we do so, I think there are no great surprises, but it is worth reflecting on just how influential these values are. It is also worth considering how deeply entrenched they are; how they are the products of a long history, in some cases reaching back through the Enlightenment and Renaissance in Europe, and further back to the Christian tradition. In this important sense, we are not a young society. And the fact we react the way we do, often in knee-jerk fashion, to killings in China or Indonesia, or to government discrimination in Malaysia or Fiji, is a product of inheriting this liberal tradition.

The potency of these liberal values in Australia, by the way, need not be an embarrassment in our relations with Asian societies. Furthermore, the message from Jakarta recently, from a very senior media figure is that it is precisely through being an exponent of these values, albeit a diplomatic exponent, that we can make a real contribution to the Asian region.

We Australians will be changing ourselves a good deal in the next few decades. In deciding where we are to go as a nation — in contemplating the idea of an Australia Foundation, for instance, it is necessary to decide the type of image of ourselves we can realistically project in the region. We need first to take stock of what we are now.

The Academy Project suggests that the very business of deepening our relations with Asia will assist us to identify the values we share. It might be argued, moreover, that these values are the necessary starting point, not only for creating a better sense of community in this country, but also for undertaking what has been called the essential micro-cultural reform of Australian society.

COMMENTARY

PUBLIC AFFAIRS DIVISION PERSPECTIVE

Richard Broinowski

The perspective from the Public Affairs Division in Canberra is somewhat different from the perspective of a regional director in Victoria. I believe that the image we project abroad is not quite as bleak as has been suggested. We have been doing systematic surveys, in Japan, Korea and Hong Kong. Frank Small, on behalf of different groups in the Federal bureaucracy, has been doing them in South-East Asia too. I would stress that there is a good deal of ignorance about Australia, but there is also a lot of positive feelings too.

We have a multi-dimensional approach towards this problem in the Federal Government. We are organising big-ticket items, such as expositions to celebrate Australia in Korea and Jakarta. For the first time we are systematically getting consultants to do professional surveys of what peoples in Asian countries think about Australia. The Overseas Information Branch and other government efforts are continuing at the same time. There is a proliferation of constructive debate around Australia about our place in Asia — the Garnaut Report, and the McKinsey Report on the 700 companies — all are indicative that, as Paul Keating has said, we are now in Asia, we are part of it.

The Federal Government is also considering a major financial commitment to promote Australian images abroad, based on constructive analysis of what we need to do to fill the gaps and plug the ignorances.

RELIGIOUS TOLERANCE

Q

India has ongoing problems caused by religious divisions. In Australia today, we are probably a very irreligious society, and yet we do tolerate and indeed assist other people to have freedom of religion. The fact that religious tolerance is something that we foster and are proud of for migrants and for those overseas should be included when we are trying to relay the better aspect of our ethics through Radio Australia.

Anthony Milner

Some of that "liberal" approach to the world that we have is shaped by Christian tradition, and it is worth reflecting on just how important that tradition has been to us. Its influence may not always have been explicitly religious but, nevertheless, the Christian tradition has shaped our thinking in such ways that lead us to have certain predictable reactions. Whether it be on East Timor, Tiannamen Square or on approaches to government in Singapore, these traditions may be significant. The positive ways in which the religious tradition has influenced concepts and values in this country is probably quite strong.

Alison Broinowski

In recent times the ABC religion unit has taken an ecumenical approach across the broadest possible range — not just of Christian sects, but of other religions as well — and has therefore tried much more than it did in the past to serve all sorts of religious communities in Australia. According to rumours in the press, this development is now under threat. And that threat, of course, would extend into Radio Australia, which would be very sad.

Australian missionaries have been active in Asian countries for a long time, and the results of their work have been both positive and negative. The positive is an amazing degree of familiarity with cultures and languages, that has grown up in the minds of Australian missionaries. In Korea we found a reunion of the Presbyterian missionaries who had established the Presbyterian Church in Korea 100 years ago, all of them Australians speaking fluent Korean. (And much better than most of us do in the foreign service.)

The negative perhaps relates more to the past than the present. I found, when I was doing research for *The Yellow Lady*, that earlier this century, missionaries would come back and deliver sermons in Australia designed to raise more money for the missions by stressing the barbarity and terrible task of living among the heathen. These missionaries would come back and raise hellfire among Australian congregations leaving very powerful impressions on the minds of the kids in the pews. But this image of the deserving poor of Asia still tends to be promulgated by the non-government organisations in their appeals for funds such as for orphans in Indonesia.

FOREIGN MEDIA

Q

I work for the *Nihon Keizai Shimbun*, the Japanese economic journal, in their Sydney bureau. My role is to put the Australian perspective to our Japanese bureau chiefs. The Australian Department of Foreign Affairs and Trade has recently improved their contact with our office. There are other Japanese newspapers and news organisations in Sydney. Perhaps Australians could be more aware of foreign media, particularly Asian media in Australia.

Alison Broinowski

Australians are much more aware now of the papers like the *Nihon Keizai Shimbun* than they ever were. At last we are getting people who can actually pronounce it correctly, which is an improvement indeed. You hear the Nikkei ("Nik-A") Index at last described as such on the ABC instead of "Nik-I", which it used to be. Also articles are taken from the Nikkei and repeated in the *Financial Review*. What has happened since 1987 when Foreign Affairs amalgamated with Trade is that we have suddenly acquired a domestic agenda. Not only has the Cold War come to an end, so all that politico-strategic stuff we used to do is much less emphasised. We now talk trade, all the time. We have a new vocabulary!

REGIONAL HEADQUARTERS IN AUSTRALIA

Kim Santow

On the subject of regional headquarters, the present Australian Government in its pre-election speech talked about dealing with incentives for regional headquarters on a case-by-case basis. But one of the things that Singapore has taught us is that ad hockery does not work. Regional headquarters must be a critical element in creating the arterial links between Australia and Asia. By that I mean that if a multinational group sets up in Australia to run its food operations throughout Asia, it will create a natural flow of people and knowledge in both directions. It does not mean, of course, that because that operation is managerial Australia has any right to expect to manage Asia. But what it does mean is that Australia will participate, and one of the greatest difficulties at the moment is that the Australian Government has not faced up to the fact they need to think through a set of competitive tax treatment measures which will allow us to say to a multinational group — you do not automatically have to go to Singapore.

Pamela Gutman

The service industries have been pushing this for some time and regional headquarters are a very good way of Australia becoming a mediator in many ways between the rest of the world and our own region, given our history and geographical position.

VI

DIPLOMATIC AND POLITICAL TIES WITH ASIA

INTRODUCTION

Christine Dobbin

The discussion in this section is led by Tim McDonald, the director of the Research Institute for Asia and the Pacific at Sydney University. The Institute was founded in its present form four years ago, to coordinate inter-disciplinary research on that region and also to make that research available to a wider community. None of this research would have been possible without the eruption into Australian academic life of a group of Asian specialists in the late 1950s and early 1960s. They had to start from a shaky institutional base. Sakuko Matsui has mentioned (p 37) how very tiny in 1961 the Japanese and Chinese Language Departments were at Sydney University. Alison Broinowski has described in her chapter how in Adelaide she studied Asia on her own. The people who inspired all of us were particular individuals, ploughing what I now, as a Sydney graduate, realise must have been a very lonely furrow indeed. I wish to pay particular tribute to a former Women's College student, Emeritus Professor Marjorie Jacobs, who somehow smuggled something on India into the History curriculum in the Third Year of the undergraduate course at Sydney in the late 1950s. She inspired many of us with a life-long commitment to India. In fact, she went further than that. She mysteriously found out about the inauguration of the first conference ever on South-East Asian studies in Singapore at the end of 1960, and at the time when we were only thinking of summer jobs in David Jones or Anthony Horderns, she encouraged a group of us students to set off for Singapore. There, we confronted our real future.

Tim McDonald, before becoming director of the Research Institute for Asia and the Pacific, had a distinguished career as a diplomat, largely in our region. He was Deputy High Commissioner to India, High Commissioner to Bangladesh, High Commissioner to Singapore, and also Minister to Washington; so he spanned both sides of the Pacific and also the Indian Ocean.

The chapter following is by Dr Rodney Tiffen, whose field of expertise is the Asian media. Rodney Tiffen is an associate professor in the Department of Government and Public Administration at the University of Sydney.

A Journey through Australia's Regional Diplomacy

Tim Mcdonald

In a talk to the Australian Institute of International Affairs, in March 1993, Gareth Evans (Australian Foreign Minister) said:
> Australian Foreign Policy has been driven by a carefully defined sense of national interest, conducted with a realistic appreciation of the scope of our influence, focussed and realistically selective in character and effective in achieving results and in building in to the process a positive image of Australia as a diplomatically active country, conducting a responsible foreign policy with imagination and energy.

Here we have a description of a well-articulated foreign policy. The test we need to apply is: is it succeeding? Owen Glendower in *Henry IV* Part 1, (another Welsh rogue if you like) boasts, "I can call spirits from the vasty deep". Prince Hal replies "Aye, will they come?". A quick journey through Australia's diplomatic history may allow us to make some judgements as to how far we have come and where we need to go in managing a successful Asian policy.

Australia's history of diplomatic and political involvement with the Asian region is very recent, dating effectively from World War II. In those early post-war years, less than 50 years ago, with Ben Chifley as Prime Minister and HG Evatt as Foreign Minister, Asia was characterised by colonial rule. Australia's response to the post-war world was an almost total identification with European and British recovery, and to maintaining and extending major alliances including retaining the colonial presences, particularly British, in the region. It also sought to protect the interests of smaller nations within the context of a vision of collective security under the auspices of the United Nations.

There was more than some ambivalence towards the process of decolonisation and much of our diplomacy was still conducted through Whitehall. Paramount in the eyes of the government of that time was the necessity to maintain Australia as a white European nation in the context of a very rapidly changing regional situation.

1950S AND 1960S — EARLY POST-WAR PERIOD

From the 1950s until the late 1960s, our policy agenda was driven by new developments arising from the immediate post war chaos: the Korean War, the Japanese Peace Treaty, the strengthening of nationalist movements in the region, the French war in Indo-China, Confrontasi, Vietnam and decolonisation. New states which were politically and economically weak emerged. These developments were seen as posing a strategic threat to Australian security. Thus our diplomatic and political ties with the region were dictated largely by strategic concerns such as Communist aggression and subversion, and threats to political stability to these young and inexperienced regimes.

Our first experience of independent interaction with the region was based largely on a global strategic perspective of a monolithic communist threat centred on the Sino-Soviet alliance. Our policy was to develop the doctrine of forward defence, using Asia as the shield against strategic threats. We became directly involved in many of the military conflicts in the region, in Korea, in Vietnam and in Malaysia. We sought to maintain British (and to an extent French and Dutch) involvement in regional defence. We were involved in the Geneva agreements, which settled the first of the Indo-China wars in 1954. It was essentially a construct of the great powers, and lasted a very short time. We were also intent on maintaining United States military power within the region. One of our principal efforts within the context of the Vietnam War was to tie America into a lasting military commitment in the region.

Our efforts to promote political stability in the region saw our ambivalence during the immediate post war period give way to a perception of the inevitability of decolonisation and a search for ways to control that process. At the same time there was a rapid build up of Australian diplomatic relations in the region and an increasing capacity for assessment of developments in the region independent of Whitehall. This period ushered in the Colombo Plan for Technical Assistance, and saw the beginning of the era of substantial development aid to the region.

In the 1950s and 1960s we were beginning to use Australia's industrial base as a supplier of manufactures to the region and as a source of investment. It is sobering to reflect now that in 1965, Australia exported more motor vehicles to Indonesia than did Japan. There was also the beginning of the development of a more liberal immigration policy in Australia.

LATE 1960S TO EARLY 1980S — CHANGED STRATEGIC OUTLOOK

From the late 1960s until the early 1980s, the strategic outlook changed radically: the British withdrawal from the region; President Nixon's Guam Doctrine ennunciated in 1969 with its emphasis on self reliance in defence; the Sino-Soviet split; internal changes in China and in perceptions of Chinese foreign policies. There was a strengthening of political and economic regimes in South-East Asia, and a growing authority and confidence among their governments. This period also saw greater political cohesion and influence grow amongst the states of South-East Asia with the formation of regional organisations such as ASEAN (the Association of South-East Asian Nations). Following the defeat of the United States in Vietnam., refugees became a regional issue and Australia became heavily involved in finding solutions on a regional basis. Japan began to emerge as a major economic power and there was a growing sense of regional identity, founded on the success of market-oriented economies. There was the beginning of the search for regional solutions to political problems, not only the refugees, but the whole Cambodian problem. This was driven by the new-found confidence of the ASEAN nations, with the great powers content to accept their political lead.

There was strong economic growth in North-East Asia: while Japan flourished, Korea and Taiwan began to flex their economic muscles as did Hong Kong. There was the beginning of the transformation of Singapore and Malaysia to industrial economies.

Australia's policy responses included the development of diplomatic relations with China and Hanoi and regional defence initiatives to fill the gap left by the departure of the British. This saw the formation of the Five Power Defence Arrangements between Australia, New Zealand, Singapore, Malaysia and the United Kingdom. Australia initiated programs of defence cooperation with the region, and broadened its political and economic relations with regional countries. The Whitlam Government finally buried "White Australia", signed a Treaty of Trade, Commerce and Friendship with Japan, and initiated a dialogue with ASEAN. The short-lived, (and not well-conceived), Regional Commonwealth Initiative was an attempt by the Fraser Government to form a regional organisation of which Australia was a natural member. These efforts were designed to engage Australia in a wider context with the region, to extend dialogue with countries in the region, as well as seeking regional solutions to problems. We saw the growth of Asian immigration, partly stemming from the refugee problem, and the adoption in Australia of "multiculturalism".

There was support for the development of regional institutions such as the Asian Development Bank, and the promoting of political stability through aid and economic growth. At the same time Australia began to project its concerns over human rights, with Timor an important stimulus. As the agenda in the region shifted, our policy responses were aimed at a broadening of the relationship from its preoccupation with strategic and defence issues.

From the early 1980s to the present, changes have been dramatic. They have transformed the agenda from what it was in the first 30 years of Australia's independent diplomacy.

Japan has become a major global economic power and exporter of capital; North-East Asia has become the fastest growing economic region in the world. There has been boom in South-East Asia, fuelled by Japanese investment, following the 1985 Plaza Accord between the United States and Japan, which revalued the Japanese yen, and an immense growth in intra-regional trade. The Asia/Pacific region has become an important economic trading region in its own right. The end of the Cold War has seen the withdrawal of Soviet power and the decline of confrontation within the region based on Cold War perceptions. There has been the triumph of market-oriented policies over doctrines of central planning in China, Vietnam and the smaller countries of Indo-China, and they have joined those institutions which they had denied in earlier times as manifestations of capitalist rule.

At the same time, there has been the emergence of a new middle class of affluent Asians, and a relative decline in Australia's wealth and power. In Singapore 10 years ago, the Singapore per capita income was about half that of Australia, and the value of the Singapore dollar was about S$2.20 = A$1.00. Ten years later, the Singapore per capita income is just shading Australia and the Australian dollar is worth almost exactly the equivalent of the Singapore dollar. As a result of these developments and the beginnings of a generational change in leadership, there is growing strength and confidence in regional governments. There is political evolution towards greater freedom and democracy in Korea, Taiwan, Thailand and the Philippines. Emerging are more open democratic systems, perhaps not as open and democratic as we might like, but nevertheless a considerable advance on what they had endured before.

POLICY RESPONSES

How has Australia responded to these enormous changes?

First of all, there has been a redefinition of our strategic doctrine, and the abandonment of forward defence. The Defence White Paper of 1987 marked significant change in our posture and defence priorities, and our interaction with the region.

We moved towards comprehensive engagement, or enmeshment, with Asia. Gareth Evans' statement of December 1989 on comprehensive engagement and the strategic bases of Australia's relationships with the region attempted to define a regional political role for Australia, and to include Australia as an integral part of that region.

Domsetically there was internationalisation of the Australian economy, financial deregulation and the lowering of tariffs. This was largely a response to international developments.

There was a reorientation of Australian trade towards Asia. The McKinsey Report on Austrade urged the need to concentrate trade and marketing resources in Asia, and away from North America and Europe where it had been traditionally placed. Growth in exports, and particularly, a dramatic growth in the exports of manufacturers to Asia, has occurred over the past six or seven years.

The connection between the internationalisation of the Australian economy, the lowering of tariffs, the freeing up of the financial system and the success in the development of exports in manufactures is important.

The promotion of regional economic cooperation through Australia's Asia Pacific Economic Cooperation (APEC) initiative, and the formation of the Cairns Group of Agricultural Producing Countries to act as means for regional dialogue, and also as a lobby group in the world dialogue on trade matters, were a part of our attempts to engage with the region, as was our initiative to promote a regional dialogue on defence. At first they met with scepticism and opposition, both from within the region and from the United States, but they are now being embraced.

Our closer involvement with the resolution of regional political issues also engendered confidence in being accepted as a regional player. Our early attempts to do so in the Cambodian issue were ineffective, even ham fisted. Later a more professional approach was adopted with considerable success.

At the same time, there was a very important development of Australian institutions for stimulating wider interaction with the region: the Australia Abroad Council, the Australia Indonesia Institute, the Australia China Council, the Australia Japan

Foundation, and more recently the initiative for an Asia Economic Centre, a special centre to study Asia and to be part of a network with regional think-tanks which influence policy development.

Prime Minister Paul Keating said in a speech to the Sydney Institute earlier this year, "Everything else we do in this country depends on our success as a trading nation". This represented a redefinition of Australian priorities in international affairs as the development of Australia's capacity as a successful trading nation. It is that proposition which now informs our regional policy, as it does our overall foreign policy, and which links foreign and domestic policies. The judgement of the Keating Government will ultimately rest on the extent to which it is able to impose on an insular bureaucracy, not to say electorate, that understanding of the connection between domestic and foreign policy and its ability to effect primarily the transition from a relationship with the region based on strategic and defence concerns to one based on economic concerns.

From this brief overview of the development of our relations over the past 40 years, what are the lessons to be learnt?

The role of foreign policy is to protect and promote the national interest. Diplomacy is its instrument. Where those interests collide with those of others, it is the function of diplomacy to seek to reconcile them or at least avoid confrontation.

In this respect the conduct of Australia's foreign policy since World War II has been unremarkable and not fundamentally different from any other country. While all countries tend to regard their situation and circumstances as unique, Australia has more than its share of policy circles which need to be squared. There is an unusually wide gap between our predominant ethnic and cultural makeup, including our political culture and those of the region where we exist.

This is not unique in the world, but we have it in a particular measure and we share it with countries like Israel, whose fate we do not particularly want to emulate as a country surrounded by a sea of hostile neighbours. Our strategic environment is South-East Asia and the Pacific, but our principal strategic alliance is with the United States. We are an insular country in the strict as well as the popular definition of the term. We have never had to deal closely with neighbours on our borders; we are unused to the complications of living next to foreigners; we are unused to having to learn what makes them tick, what informs their mind, why they see the world differently to us. Our nearest neighbours for practical purposes are several thousand miles from our urban conglomerates around our coastline.

Historically, we have sought to conduct an outward-looking defence policy with an inward-looking economic policy. The reversal of this in the mid-1980s, has left us perplexed. In less than 40 years, our external economic relations have not only shifted from a basis of over 50 percent with Europe, principally Britain, to over 50 percent with Asia, but the framework within which that trade was conducted in our earlier history with its Empire preferences has not been replaced by a comparable regional trading arrangement. The region's experience in terms of independent diplomacy is very limited. There are no deep historical roots of diplomacy such as there are in Europe on which to draw in solving our problems. Factors such as these tend to undermine our confidence in dealing with foreign policy issues. We have to learn to be more confident in our dealings with the region, but how to do it?

Until the mid 1980s, Australian policy towards the region centred on defence and strategic issues. In the policy confusion of the late 1960s and 1970s built on the shifting sands of the minerals boom, we missed the opportunity to be, to use the title of Dean Acheson's memoirs, "present at the creation" of the Asian boom now reaching its full flowering. Instead we turned inwards. We raised tariffs, we turned much of our manufacturing industry into a museum exhibit. The base from which we might have become part of the dynamism of the region, was eroded. We debated the distribution of the decreasing pool of national wealth while our neighbours were single-mindedly focused on creating it. We relied on Asia only for that in which we could not be self sufficient — that is to say, defence.

Little wonder then that there has been scepticism about our new found commitment to internationalising our economy and our motives for comprehensive engagement. A quarter of a century after the White Australia Policy was abandoned, its spectre still haunts our relations with the region, at least at a popular level. I fear it will take as long a time to recover from what for us was the equivalent of Mao's cultural revolution in China — two lost decades of opportunity. We are all guilty — Foreign Affairs, of which I was part, as much as any because many there understood the problems at first hand. I recall 15 years ago when Dick Boyer, formerly with the Tariff Commission, was a lonely voice crying in the wilderness about protectionism. He was a fellow in the Department of Foreign Affairs, and sought to have it lead a crusade for more enlightened policies, but we turned our backs on him.

THE LESSONS

What this illustrates is the importance of a sound domestic policy base for a successful foreign policy. As we become more experienced, we also have to learn that there is more to foreign policy-making than the projections of one's domestic policy priorities on to the international scene, as we did in the early stages of the Cambodian problem and still do in handling human rights issues.

We have to have a much more professional understanding of the strategic priorities in the region and the strategic framework within which our policies operate.

This means that we need a high level of professionalism at the political level as well as within the bureaucracy in the conduct of our foreign policy. That in turn means a better informed electorate and political process and improving the level of debate about our relationship with the region and how we identify with it.

It is an inescapable characteristic of participatory democracies that we are constantly confronted with false dichotomies. We are told (even on the authority of the Prime Minister in his Sydney Institute Speech) that in order to improve our trade performance, and I quote him, "we must increasingly become part of Asia".

The people, as Hugh Mackay's research has revealed, are rightly sceptical of such simplistic notions.

Australia is neither geographically nor culturally part of Asia. What we can claim is that we are a significant trader, a strategic factor and a political player in the Asia Pacific region. This raises an important but rather more difficult question of how well we are performing that function. We do not need to deny our cultural heritage, but we do have to understand the region and its many cultures better if we are to make the most of the enormous opportunities which developments there have opened up.

There are two vital things we must understand: the first is that these countries too are undergoing major transformations, and are redefining their own societies. At the same time there is emerging some sense of regional identity, as yet ill defined, but premised on the economic success of the past two decades and the growth of interaction among its members. The second is that it is international pluralism that provides the political framework for Asia Pacific cooperation. This presents both an opportunity and a challenge for diplomacy. Part of the redefinition of Australian society must surely take into account the changes going on around us. It provides us with the opportunity to harmonise the choices we make with those of the region, where, for the first time in our history, all our vital interests — strategic, political, social (including immigration) and economic — are most strongly engaged. Australians should be comforted, if not flattered, by the degree of interest shown by the media of the region in the republican debate.

We should be relieved to learn that the assertion that we have somehow to change the very basis of our cultural heritage into something more "Asian" is false. The challenge lies in our accepting pluralism for what it is, and to work with it without surrendering our basic values, but tempering their projection into the political backyards of our neighbours.

Ross Garnaut, in his 1992 Sir Hermann Black Lecture, noted:

> Australia suffers from East Asian, especially South-East Asian, perceptions of Australia as an international busy body, specialising in the gratuitous insult to other societies and politics, maintaining a raucous critique of other countries' political cultures and systems.

He went on to argue that international commerce, which is growing faster here than anywhere else in the world, transmits political as well as economic information and values, and that learning the regional virtues of patience is the beginning of wisdom in this respect.

There are other lessons that we must learn. There is a huge challenge before us, given the diversity of cultures in our region and the gulf which exists between them and the foundations of European culture which informs ours so heavily.

The burden of closing these gaps must fall again on an education system already overburdened with solving society's problems. But this is a question of national survival, at least at the standard to which we have become accustomed, and as such deserves some priority. Not only does a successful foreign policy, especially in a participatory democracy, ultimately rest on a well-informed public, but let us not kid ourselves, diplomacy is really the only weapon we have. We lack the political, economic, the industrial and the military clout to impose our interests on the region. We have to use our brains, our intellect and our persuasive capacity to advance our interests there.

A better cultural understanding of the region is a sore necessity. Popular perceptions of Australia in Asia are 20 years out of date and the reverse stereotypes in Asia about Australia are almost as laughable and damaging as our stereotypes about them. Our diplomacy needs to be supported by major cultural and information program.

What I suggest is that an important part of the change which is now taking place in Australia and the redefinition of our society extends well beyond our shores. Part of that challenge brings us face to face with some fundamental issues as well as with some outstanding opportunities. The luck of the lucky country is not yet exhausted. We happen to be part of the most dynamic economic region in the world. Whether we use that lucky break or dissipate it is the question which history will answer for us.

Regional Relations: The Politics of Continuing Change

Rodney Tiffen

There is a bit of a nostalgic revival of the Robert Menzies' period at the moment, especially on the Liberal side of politics, (because Menzies could do something very well that they cannot, namely win elections). It might be worth looking at the pattern of Menzies' overseas trips when he was Prime Minister for the 16 years from 1949. During that time he made 20 official visits as Prime Minister and only two of these, the two shortest, involved visits to Asian countries without going on to the United States or the United Kingdom. Menzies made 17 visits to Britain, 16 to the United States and 8 to Canada. In contrast, he made 1 visit to Indonesia, 1 visit to the Philippines, 1 visit to Malaysia and Singapore and 2 to Thailand. In total, a ratio of 41 visits to the 3 North Atlantic countries, and 6 to the ASEAN countries — almost a 7 to 1 ratio. It is also notable that in the year after Sir Robert ceased being Prime Minister, Japan became our biggest trading partner and in his 16 years as Prime Minister, he had but paid 2 visits to Japan. The disproportion became worse the longer Menzies was Prime Minister. In fact from 1960 to 1965, the Prime Minister's only land fall in Asia was a stopover in Bangkok returning from London.

Let me be bipartisan about this: what about the Labor side? I recall a somewhat nasty passage in Gough Whitlam's memoirs where as Deputy Leader of the Labor Party, he was about to fly off to Asia for some conference, and just as he was going, Arthur Calwell said to Margaret Whitlam — "I'm glad it's him and not me. You never know what you'll catch over there". In fact it is also worth recalling that in 1950 when we were setting up an embassy in Jakarta, Arthur Calwell spoke against it as an unnecessary thing to do in what was really a very insignificant part of the earth's surface.

These attitudes also existed among some of our diplomats at that time. I have recently discovered, in a student thesis in our department, a memo from the Australian Ambassador to Indonesia in 1958. His response to an Indonesian Dance Troupe who wanted to visit Australia, was to advise the minister to do nothing because "the Indonesians tend to be very unreliable and with any luck they'll forget about it". And I think this points to the battles that Alison Broinowski and other cultural activists had in the department over the years to say that perhaps Asian culture is worth paying some attention to.

Of course, those sorts of attitudes and priorities are well and truly in the past. But we should never forget just how far we have had to travel in such a short time. Last year, the *Australian Left Review* had what I thought was a wonderful cover, which summed up the change in the priority and attitude given to Asia almost universally amongst Australian decision-makers. It said "From Yellow Peril to Main Game".

Certainly today in Australian political and professional circles, there are far more attitudes of respect, of flexibility and of willingness to learn about Asia and from Asians , and this will continue. Asia will continue to be a dynamic region, marked by the emergence of a new middle class of affluent Asians, the growing strength and confidence of regional governments, the beginnings of a generational change of leadership and the signs of some evolution towards greater freedom and democracy in some Asian countries.

However, if the last decade has taught us anything, it is about the speed and unpredictability of change. Ten years ago, former

President Marcos seemed impregnable; indeed the whole Soviet Empire and Eastern Europe seemed impregnable. Now they are all gone. The mood in Europe a few years ago was very optimistic. But now the mood is pessimistic, induced both by several apparently insoluble conflicts and not least for economic reasons. It is worth remembering that unemployment in the EC will probably top 20 million in the next year.

So while it is true and I think it will continue to be true that we live in a very exciting and dynamic region, there are likely to be occasional sources of instability, all sorts of reverses, all sorts of unpredictabilities that should caution us against being too romantic about that dynamism. The election in Japan might change Japanese politics in that country in an unpredictable way. I quote from that great scholar and gentleman, Derryn Hinch, who used to advertise his program by saying "Expect the unexpected". I think we can still look forward to many things that we do not expect in the future in our region.

In grasping future Australian relations with the neighbouring region, it must be stressed that state to state relations are now a proportionally smaller part of the total of international relations. And related to that, national boundaries are becoming more and more porous to all sorts of transactions — to the movement of people, to the movement of commercial activities, to cultural endeavours, to the flow of information, even, of course, to criminal activities. So I think we should underline that history and technology are on the side of those who want more open frontiers, for both good and bad. And those countries which seek to define various things as their own domestic affair increasingly are on the defensive regarding historical changes.

We are confronted today not just by transnational corporations which get a lot of publicity, but by transnational NGOs (Non Government Organisations), which increasingly organise on an international basis. In fact one of the interesting things I discovered recently was a new coalition of groups for monitoring transgressions against the news media and international reporting. Groups like the human rights group, Article XIX, UNESCO, Amnesty, The International Federation of Journalists, Reporters sans Frontiers and others have formed this new group. And one of the impetuses to it of course is the fact that 35 journalists have so far been killed in former Yugoslavia — more journalists killed there than in the whole history of the Vietnam War. For the first time perhaps in any warfare, they were deliberately targeted to be killed precisely because they are journalists.

That leads me to question some aspects of the quote from Ross Garnaut in Tim McDonald's previous chapter. It would be a great mistake for us to think that human rights issues are a thing of the past. In recent years, we have seen in many Asian countries, in Thailand, in China, in the Philippines, in Burma and others, often with tragic results, that human rights are not just Western agendas imposed on Asia, they are agendas that significant and important parts of those Asian nations pursue also. Four years ago, at a memorial service at Sydney University after the massacre at Tiananmen Square, Nick Greiner, Bob Carr and all sorts of other people gave very moving speeches, as of course did Bob Hawke and others in Canberra. I think this is a sign of cultural strength on Australia's part, that our humanity did not stop at national borders, but that there was a very real sense of engagement with victims of those massacres, and a desire to take a stand. This may sometimes cause diplomatic inconvenience, but I think it is a virtue of our culture that I hope and am sure will continue to be operating into the 1990s.

I conclude by observing that government policy should recognise the pluralism of forces at work. The government itself is now only a much smaller part of the total of international relations. And one implication of that is that their calculations of pragmatism must expand to recognise the limits of the government's role. I have often argued, for example, that on East Timor, it would have been more pragmatic to pursue a consistently principled line than to get the wavering and reversing that has caused so much resentment in Indonesia. I refer to Tim McDonald's quote (p 141) from *Henry IV* "I can call spirits: from the vasty deep" — "Aye, but will they come". Another response is "but, will only *they* come?". All sorts of other spirits not called may also be coming forth in our relationships with Asia. I certainly think that we have in the next decade got the classic Chinese curse, that we certainly will be continuing to live in very interesting times.

COMMENTARY

OVERSEAS AID

Q

In the developing countries of Asia what form do you think Australian aid should take? Should it be money or services and what sort of conditions do you think Australia should apply?

Tim McDonald

We should wean our foreign policy away from any residual dependency on aid. Ideas of international aid in respect of East Asia is mostly a hangover from the thinking of the 1960s and 1970s and need to be rethought. That is not to deny that there is a place for foreign aid in objective terms as well as in terms of promotion of our interests and development of foreign policy. But I do not think it should be a fundamental consideration. I offer a personal observation here which is not strictly relevant to the question. I find it extraordinary that we spend less than a tenth of what we spend on foreign aid on our cultural and information programs to project Australia and its achievements into the world. Part of the thinking behind the aid program traditionally has been that it buys some goodwill, and gains access as a player in the economic sense. But there are more effective ways of doing both. Increasingly, aid programs are driven by a dichotomy of motives, chiefly humanitarian such as aid to Somalia and on the commercial advantage which they can provide in competing for contracts. Foreign aid has become irrelevant in countries like Singapore; in some it will mean survival, and others, for example, Indonesia where about half the development budget is still funded by foreign aid commitments it will remain signficant for development.

MUTUAL UNDERSTANDING AND TRADE RELATIONS

Q

Tim McDonald gave us a quotation from Paul Keating, "everything else we do in this country is dependent upon our success as a trading nation". I would like to ask him about the area of knowledge of Asian languages. Do we have sufficient capability in this area now to regard ourselves as being serious in taking up that challenge?

Tim McDonald

No, I think we are ill prepared for comprehensive engagement. We still have not got in place the necessary foundations to make that policy successful. What it does imply is a much greater level of interaction between the peoples and institutions of countries. The role of governments and state-to-state relations in international relations is diminishing, while the role of non-government organisations, of individuals, of business people, of corporations and of professionals is growing. This means that there is a vast network being established between peoples, and that is where you run into our inadequacy in terms of preparation for understanding the differences between ourselves and the cultures of the countries we are dealing with.

You need an understanding of their motives, the language, the social structure and cultural imperatives and thoughts which inform the people you are dealing with. As that web of interaction increases, as "comprehensive engagement or enmeshment" progresses, we are going to need more people who are at least minimally informed and who understand the cultures with which they are dealing.

The same is true for business. Our traditional exports to these countries were the big ticket items — they were wheat and commodities like coal and iron and steel. In order to sell a couple of hundred million tons of coal you probably need a negotiating team of about half a dozen people who in turn interact with about half a dozen people at the other end. But our future prosperity depends on continuing the recent strong growth in industrial manufactures. This involves thousands of different products and thousands of different firms and thousands of people interacting in a business sense in order to make it work. As we become less dependent on those big ticket items and more dependent on the sale of our manufactures, it is going to involve a whole range of Australians interacting with a whole range of people in Asian countries. We have barely made a start on training for that.

We did make an encouraging start in the 1960s and 1970s and then we tended to dissipate it. We trained a whole lot of people in Asian languages, but we did not fully have a use for them other than in academic circles. We did not use them in commerce and industry and professions, so that resource was somewhat wasted. We now must recreate it and that is another of the big challenges coming for us.

To relate that to Paul Keating's statement: unless you have the wealth in order to sustain the creation of that infrastructure, you fall further and further behind. Somehow we have to pull ourselves up by our boot straps to put investment into creating wealth in the future. That probably means hard times for another ten years while we repair the damage of the Australian cultural revolution of the 1960s and 1970s.

Rodney Tiffen

I have mixed feelings about the Hawke/Keating Governments of the past decade, but one thing in which they have succeeded, by sheer perseverance, is to change the whole culture of how we think about our role in the world and to realise that we really do need to pay our way. In that sense, I think they have been very successful. It has not always gone along so well in performance terms. Some of that is due to shortcomings in government, but, as in so many of our dealings with Asian countries, the private sector has lagged way behind the public sector. We talk about entrepreneurs, but Australian entrepreneurs are often not very entrepreneurial, especially when it involves doing things they are not used to.

MONITORING THE MEDIA

Q *(to Rodney Tiffen)*

I am interested in the international organisation for monitoring the media. We are so dependent everywhere, Australia and elsewhere, on what we learn through the media. Is there any organisation within Australia which attempts to monitor the media?

Rodney Tiffen

I think I must dash your hopes because the international organisation I referred to is more for monitoring abuses against the media, and not for monitoring, for example, how accurately or how well they are reporting. It consists of groups like the Canadian group, and the Committee to Defend Journalists. The groups that do tend to say "You got this wrong" often have very strong biases of their own. There is a group which started off, somewhat promisingly, in the United States called Accuracy in Media, but it degenerated into a far-right think tank. As far as I know, there are not any good authoritative or thorough types of institutions which consistently monitor media performance in a desirable way.

ASIAN RELATIONS AND THE AUSTRALIAN REPUBLICAN ISSUE

Q

Tim McDonald mentioned the republican issue in Australia and the perception of it by our neighbours in the near north. Has the issue in fact attracted any significant attention or mention in that area? What do they see as being the significance of it for our relationship with South-East Asia?

Tim McDonald

In a recent visit to Indonesia I was astonished to find that every day in the English language paper there was an up-to-date report on the Republican debate. It is being interpreted, possibly in a way which we would not interpret it ourselves, as an effort on the part of Australia to redefine itself in terms which are not dependent on its European culture and background. It is seen as an important step in cutting the umbilical cord to Europe and dependency on the western world and the start of a process of coming to terms with Australia's geography. That perception may or may not be accurate and it may be quite different from our intentions. It is nevertheless, an important perception. We ought to be aware of it as we proceed with the Republican debate, to redefine our political system and the sort of country we are and what our outlook on the world will be. We must also be sensitive to the conclusions we are drawing and relate them to the similar process of redefinition of societies which is going on in the region. Should we take this opportunity to bring ourselves closer in terms of our political structure and culture to one which is well understood within the region — a political system which is based on an identification of a country's own national goals, on a strong sense of nationalism, a strong sense of identity, of freeing from past bonds?

The central importance of this all this is that, in one sense, the republican debate is necessary. It is the debate we have to have. We have to go through it in order to demonstrate to ourselves, and in the secondary sense demonstrate to the region, how and why we are redefining our place in the world.

Rodney Tiffen

I agree with that. I do not have any valid data, so I guess it is projecting somewhat. But I know that when Sir John Kerr fired Gough Whitlam in 1975, this was looked on as a pretty strange sort of event through most of Asia. I feel that insofar as the debate about the Republic is serious, it is an assertion of national maturity and national independence, and it will do us good rather than harm. On the other hand, let me just give you two anecdotes from when I lived in Japan. I was rung up frantically by the national broadcaster, the NHK, the major broadcaster one day saying, "We need to do an interview with you because of the big changes in your national anthem." This was in the mid-1980s. I said "big changes, what do you mean?" I rang up the Australian embassy and it emerged that we had actually made a couple of changes — one was, we changed the opening phrase from "Australia's Sons Let Us Rejoice" to "Australians All Let Us Rejoice" and there was one other elimination of sexism. The Japanese media thought this was a very big deal and I really should go and explain this straight away. Likewise I remember a student in class asking me why is it the Southern Cross on the Australian Flag has five stars and on the New Zealand flag it only has four stars? But in truth, I had never noticed the difference. So, while I certainly would not suggest that we should in any way inhibit discussion about a movement towards a republic, I do think we should also recognise that many Asian countries are much more sensitive to symbolic changes than we might think. We must certainly manage the way we convey these changes to other countries very carefully.

HUMAN RIGHTS

Q

The link between the growth of child prostitution and tourism in the Asia-Pacific region is a vexing issue. Australia and Germany have recently taken an initiative to create laws so that they can prosecute their own citizens in other countries, but obviously this is going to be very difficult to enforce and will need a lot of international cooperation. Do you see a need for more extradition treaties with countries in the region and what are the difficulties associated with that? It is a recent phenomenon in many of these countries where there is a lack of jurisprudence protecting children. Do you see Australia as having a role in developing legislation to protect children within those countries?

Rodney Tiffen

It is certainly doing nothing for Australian relations with Asia to have these sorts of abuses going on. My only question would be about effectiveness. But insofar as international regimes of cooperation might help, I would be all in favour of them.

COMMENTARY

Tim McDonald

I think it is an issue that needs sensitive handling. It would be wrong to approach it in the way that some Australians tend to do, of taking the high moral ground. Or that we are going to lead Asia to salvation on this issue by taking some initiative. There would be a perception that we are moralising and the other governments would tend to stand back and say, "let Australia go and do its thing if it wants to". It seems to me the way to tackle an issue like this is to very quietly try generating consensus. You may not even have to take the lead. There is already action being taken by the new administration in the Philippines. Australia could pick that up and take it a little further. Sometimes in these countries, as in the environmental debate, those people with vested interests in these businesses often have influence in government. We see these issues as self-evident stark matters of principle — a wrong to be righted. But it is not always so clear cut in these societies. We have to learn to adapt to that lack of clarity in issues in Asia, and try to solve them in an Asian way by consensus, rather than confronting them.

Rodney Tiffen

We need to learn the virtue of patience — tone is as important as substance in the way that we tackle these sorts of things. We especially need to overcome our past well-deserved reputation for arrogance in these things.

Questions of otherness and sameness are a recurring theme in relations with the Asian region. This is a very delicate area. Absolute expressions about otherness in moral judgements can be offputting. Likewise, assumptions of sameness can be just as damaging. I always remember a quote from a Kansas senator in the late 1940s saying how America was going to help China: "We'll lift Shanghai up and up until it is just like Kansas City". So presumptions of sameness can be just as bad as presumptions of total otherness.

Q   (to Rodney Tiffen)

On the subject of human rights, Amnesty's Annual Report targets certain areas of Asia as a human rights black spots. Quite apart from the opportunities Asia represents for Australia, it also presumably represents a huge responsibility.

Rodney Tiffen

The present government, under Senator Evans, has probably done about as well as we can expect on human rights. More importantly, the government's prerogatives and responsibilities are not ours. It is inappropriate for academics, for journalists, for associations of concerned citizens to act as if they were governments in waiting. Governments have to handle government-to-government relationships, but that should not silence us or blind us, or in any way constrain us in speaking the truth about human rights abuses as clearly and as accurately as we can.

ASIA'S RESPONSE TO APEC

Q

Recently the Australian media was waxing lyrical about Clinton's embracing of APEC. What was the response in the Asian countries?

Tim McDonald

I have some worry that we are running too fast with APEC. It was an important initiative. There was a lot of effective diplomacy done in gathering the ASEAN countries into that consensus. I do not think we launched it quite as well as we might have, a public speech by the Prime Minister in an Asian country. We sent Richard Woolcott as secretary of Foreign Affairs around Asia to do what should have been the preliminary work afterwards. He did it very effectively, so the ASEAN countries were brought into the consensus, but they are still a bit wary of it. The Thai Prime Minister was quoted recently as saying he did not understand what APEC was all about and the Malaysian Prime Minister has said he will not go to the summit, and others have reservations. It is something we have got to progress fairly carefully.

COMMENTARY

We have to understand that things tend to move in Asia through relationships rather than through institutions. The important thing about APEC is to use that framework to start building up those relationships to the point where foreign ministers, trade ministers, and finance ministers can pick up the phone and talk to each other about regional problems. We should not rush the institutional development. Keating and Clinton, both new to foreign policy, are the sort who want to lead from the front. That is not always the Asian way. There is also an inclination in the western cultural tradition to build monuments. There are dangers is this type of leadership that we might tear APEC apart through giving it too much momentum too early.

VII

AUSTRALIAN AND ASIAN LITERATURE

INTRODUCTION

Robin Marsden

In Australia and in the region which we inhabit, we look to our artists for illumination, for other ways of seeing. They bear witness to transformation in the forms of art which they choose. Professor Pierre Ryckmans and Professor Yasmine Gooneratne are two quite remarkable people: artists whose work has arisen from, drawn on and crossed various cultures. Both are deeply cultivated in the English literary tradition and utterly masterful as writers of English prose. They belong to a band of writers of non-English origins, internationally known and internationally acclaimed, who choose to play upon the instrument of language in English. To hear them play upon that instrument, we who are native speakers are enriched and learn more about our own language. Pierre Ryckmans and Yasmine Gooneratne have been drawn to the instrument of the English language for its resources in the expression of thought. Thought is never divorced from its expression; the process is organic. They are at home in English.

The work of Pierre Ryckmans or Simon Leys, his literary pseudonym, has been familiar to me for many years now. And I know I am not the only reader who has turned to him in troubled times for considerable illumination. Pierre's thinking is original and challenging, as elegant as the prose he writes, in French or in English. His students in Chinese have been inspired by his thought and by his example. Some of his students, including Geremie Barmé, are already making a quite invaluable contribution to our perceptions of China. Many of you will have read Simon Leys' *Chinese Shadows*[1] and will have appreciated the passionate understanding of China's political complexities and realities that has informed it. The range of Pierre Ryckmans' writings published here and overseas will astonish you. At the moment Pierre is Professor of Chinese at Sydney University. If you have not yet read his prize-winning novel, *Death of Napoleon*,[2] in French or in English, I suggest you do it immediately. It is not a lengthy read, but it will echo down the memory for a long time afterwards. The style quivers with wit and with the underlying sadness of irony.

Yasmine Gooneratne is another Australian writer who draws students to her and sends them out into the world equipped with an informed discernment that arises, so I am told, from a shared enjoyment of English literature, particularly of the works of Jane Austen. Her emphasis is on a joyful understanding of inspired writing. Recently I have been consulting some of Yasmine's former students who have told me how much they carry with them of her responses to the works they have studied with her. Her own writings spring from a love of English literature that has everything to do with becoming part of a great tradition. As in the case of Pierre Ryckmans, it is obvious when one reads Yasmine's books that they too resonate with her sense of the depth of that tradition. Also in Yasmine's case, there is that enthusiasm, a tremendous openness to what is happening to her. The clarity of mind and humour that she brings to bear on the study of English texts are part of her style in her creative writing. Her words carry with them riches from the past, from her Sri Lankan origins and her academic life and become memorable for the reader because of the unique transmutations that have taken place. Yasmine is not only Professor of English at Macquarie University but also the author of several published works, the latest *A Change of Skies*.[3] Her chapter examines images of Asia in Australian literature.

Asia in the Australian Literary Imagination

Yasmine Gooneratne

This chapter will look at "Images of Asia" from the point of view of an academic and a writer. I am perhaps that non-existent person, an "Asian", though I should probably have an image problem about that, after a photographer on an Adelaide newspaper, needing to photograph the author of a novel about a Sri Lankan English professor and his wife on a visit to Australia, chose the doorway of a Lebanese take-away on Cleveland Street, Sydney as an appropriate location.

Another scenario — and this is one that runs practically every year — features a classroom in which a university academic in a sari is giving a lecture on Goldsmith, or Dr Johnson, or Jane Austen. A student comes in late, looks around, says "Oops, sorry, wrong lecture", and departs. Maybe he or she expected to see at the lectern some six-foot-tall, pipe-smoking, tweeded, and possibly bearded male. And nowadays, of course, as Australian films make a breakthrough abroad, they create a problem of a slightly different kind. I was in the United States two years ago, as Visiting Professor of English at the University of Michigan. The son of my host, brought over by his father to meet "the Australian professor", told him *sotto voce*, "Gee, dad, she doesn't look like Paul Hogan".

When I was asked to put together some ideas on Australian literary images of Asia, unwittingly the request hit on the central theme of a novel I am now writing. The inspiration for that novel comes, I should say — as most of my good ideas do come — from my husband, whose collection of world maps I have been recently cataloguing. I was particularly interested in two 18th century maps, one by Gerard van Keulen and the other by Matthaei Seutteri, which created a chain of ideas. It is the sort of thing, I find, that happens to novelists. They start out on a seemingly straightforward project, and without warning find themselves in the midst of a story.

Maps are, in any case, very important, for when we are proposing to enter unknown territory (whether it is a town, a country, the mind of a society — or even a republic), we tend to look to maps and map-makers for guidance, for clues, for a reliable image of the unknown land. But map-makers are themselves creators of potent and durable images. Bharat, one of the characters in my novel *A Change of Skies*,[1] discovers this early on, as he thinks about the tiny store of knowledge about Australia that he has accumulated through childhood and youth:

> The word "Australia" summoned up in my mind a single picture, one which I instantly recognised as having come straight out of the *Philip's Atlas* I had used as a schoolboy at Royal. On Philip's map of the world, huge areas of the earth's surface had broken out in the rash of washed-out pink patches which denoted British ownership. To the east of India and the island of Ceylon (also pink), south of Borneo and Sarawak, there Australia had been, a blank pink space shaped like the head of a Scotch terrier with its ears pricked up and its square nose permanently pointed westwards, towards Britain.
>
> That doggy devotion to Britain is something that I, familiar with the colonial traditions of my own family, fully understand the reasons for, even though I do not, of course, personally subscribe to it.[2]

It occurred to me that many people who refer to "Asia" do so as if they are talking about something quite alien to Australian history and sensibility, something quite "other". They may not have intended to do so, but that is the way it comes across. I have now lived in Australia for 21 years, and I often hear Asia referred to in this way. But as an Australian who was born and partly educated in an Asian country that was at one time, like Australia, a British colony, it does not cease to surprise me.

This being the case, I want to enter the world of contemporary literature by casting back to the past. I shall begin with a reminder that Australia's colonial experience was shared with many of the free nations of modern Asia. In common with India, Sri Lanka, Burma, Malaysia and Singapore, Australia had a place, as Salman Rushdie puts it memorably in his article "The New Empire in Britain", in that large part of the map of the world which blushed a rosy pink as it writhed pleasurably under the weight of the British Empire. In common with these nations, Australia inherited a Westminster-style Constitution and a British-style education dispensed, naturally, through the English language, and standardised with the greatest efficiency and thoroughness.

There was, however, an important difference. English education in Asia was carried out in the light of Thomas Babington Macaulay's ignorant, simple-minded but enormously influential prejudice against the civilisations of Asia. Macaulay had stated in his *Minute on Indian Education*[3] in 1835:

> The question now before us is simply whether, when it is in our power to teach (English), we shall teach languages in which, by universal confession, there are no books on any subject which deserve to be compared with our own; whether, when we can teach European science, we shall teach systems which, whenever they differ from those of Europe, differ for the worse; and whether, when we can patronise sound Philosophy and true History we shall countenance, at the public expense, medical doctrines which would disgrace an English farrier; Astronomy, which would move laughter in girls in an English boarding-school; History, abounding with Kings thirty feet high; and Geography, made up of seas of treacle and seas of butter.

Macaulay was a poet as well as a historian, and it is easy to see how powerful and influential the effect of the denigratory images he deliberately uses here must have been, about a subject of which he knew — as he freely admitted — almost nothing!

Settler-type colonies such as Australia, that presented no indigenous literature with which British educationists had to contend, inherited an English education of the type dispensed in Britain. They also inherited Macaulayan attitudes to Asia. Since words are the tools that writers use, and Australians for the most part use English words in their literary expression, I thought it might be useful, first, to take a look at some of the images of Asia that have become part of the Australian mental framework through an English-language education.

To glance briefly at three authors who were staples of English literary education in colonial schools during the 19th century:

1. Shakespeare. Texts that were often taught in schools and universities were: *The Merchant of Venice* with its portrait of an evil-minded Jewish miser and money-lender; *The Tempest*, with its picture of colonised islanders insulted, punished and completely dominated by a beneficent ruler from the West; *Julius Caesar*, with its stirring evidence that traitors and conspirators, however noble in spirit, must come to a sticky end; and *Anthony and Cleopatra*, with its portrait of a woman who embodied in her powerful sexuality all that the Western world most feared and distrusted in the "Orient".
2. James Thomson's *The Seasons*,[4] especially "Winter", with its portrait of Peter of Russia, the barbarian king who learns cultivated manners in Europe, and goes back to educate his people.
3. Wordsworth's "Daffodils", a poem so universally taught that DJ Enright, poet, professor and publisher, claimed there had been an identifiable period during which every child of a certain age throughout the British Empire, whether that child was resident in Africa, Canada, India or Australia, was reciting it in class. If I may introduce a personal note here, I'd like to say that though it is one of my own favourites among Wordsworth's poems, many of my Australian students have told me they have had problems with Wordsworth's daffodils because daffodils do not grow naturally in Australia, and with Shakespeare's daffodils because in Australia they certainly do not "come before the swallow dares" and take "the winds of March with beauty".

So we have here examples of texts that are culturally disorienting in some cases, culturally stereotyping in others. I have prepared for my students a mini-anthology of extracts from standard English literature texts in which allusions to Asia occur. What interests me in these passages, especially when put into an historical perspective, is the way the romantic, exotic images of Asia as a paradise of "gold and Orient pearle", "pleasant fruits and princely delicates", the home of "worldly treasures and pleasures", filled with spices and mines full of rubies, that dominated the pre-colonial period, give way to images of a quite different kind after Europe began its big push into Asia from the 16th century on.

Gradually we can see a 19th century view emerging in the West which emphasised the backwardness of Asia and its stubborn resistance to the spread of the Christian and Western way of life. This was the code which provided justification for European peoples to define their national character as strong both physically and in matters of moral fibre, virtuous and brave, measuring it constantly against an exotic, alien, sometimes sinister, always fascinating "other" — Asia.

It is not especially surprising to me, given such a deep-rooted training in cultural prejudice, that, despite their geographical location, which gave Australians a chance to become the world's best informed English-speaking authorities on Asia, they appear to have accepted in the past what Alison Broinowski calls "Europe's Orientalist constructs" as substitutes for knowledge.[5] It would seem that today many Australians would accept equally unquestioningly Asian stereotypes fabricated by the American media.

Australia's earliest attitudes towards Asia were certainly inherited ones, the legacy of a Europe which had made its first contact with Asia around the 14th century (see also Jacqueline Menzies' chapter, pp 194-196). A powerful image of a cultural "penetration" of the East by the superior strength of Western ideas and technology has been the focus for many hundreds of years of Western literary renderings of the East-West encounter. It is no accident that the subject has so frequently been presented in terms of a central image of sexual embrace doomed to end in sorrow and separation, with the West as "hero" strong in virtue, and the East cast in the "weaker" and "beguiling" (feminine) role. Writers and others involved in the arts would be especially sensitive to such powerfully influential works as Shakespeare's drama *Antony and Cleopatra* and Puccini's opera *Madame Butterfly* which gave this perception classic treatment, while such novels and films as *Bhowani Junction*, *Sayonara*, and *South Pacific* have rendered it in terms of popular cinema.

Australians, like other colonials East and West, North and South, were eager consumers of the images that flooded Australia from the source of culture and knowledge: imperial Britain. With the establishment of Empire, the image (general in British literature throughout the 16th, 17th and 18th centuries) of Asia as a source of unparalleled mystery, beauty, dignity and wealth, the source of mathematical knowledge, religious philosophy, and the most delicate (or, alternatively, the most sensual) art, had to give way to an image that was more *controllable*, one that justified the British imperial presence in the East.

Its place was taken by the image of Asians as childlike, in need of moral education and political guidance from a Crown that saw itself, presumably, as something like a strict but kindly English nanny. In a pub in Perth a few years ago I encountered an elderly gentleman who was able to recite from memory the whole of Kipling's poem *Gunga Din*, a vigorous, energetic piece of writing that is written from the viewpoint, and in the idiom of, a British Tommy Atkins who, when he is done with belting his Indian bearer and insulting him verbally and in every other way, grants him generously the accolade: "You're a better man than I am, Gunga Din!" (Of course, the bearer had to die first, shot down in the act of loyally bringing water to his master, who was lying wounded and helpless on an Indian battlefield.) The stories and poems of Kipling, and the popular songs of Noel Coward helped to shape the Australian point of view, partly because as literature they were so memorable and well written, partly because familiarity with them encouraged the Australian to *join in*, to stop feeling an excluded colonial, and become "one of the lads"; and partly because they were such jolly good fun: Coward sang of a world among the dangers and perils of which the Englishman proved his innate superiority by riding mysteriously unscathed. In that imperial world, in so many tropical parts of which: "Mad dogs and Englishmen go out in the midday sun".

It is hardly surprising, then, that such potent images as these, of sinister, lazy, cowardly, bestial and incompetent "Orientals", took deep root in the Australian literary and artistic imagination.

Times, however, seem to be a-changing. Australia's emergence as a nation officially independent of Britain in 1901, her participation in two world wars (and several more localised ones), and the arrival here and settlement of immigrants from many parts of the world including Asia, have introduced modifications in the accepted West/East way of looking at the contemporary world. The experiences of Australians from many walks of life who have travelled, lived and worked in Asia over many years have modified it further. With the emergence of Japan and other Pacific nations as economic and technological forces in the 1980s, the pattern has changed yet again. It seems to me that the prospects for growth in Australian literature arising out of an improved knowledge of Asia and an understanding of Asian literary traditions, are better now than they were in earlier years, and are improving every day. The delicate short story writing of Mena Abdullah, Australian writer of Punjabi origin, has managed to stay in print in Australia for nearly 30 years. *The Time of the Peacock*[6] has been a textbook in Australian primary schools, and I have met several students in whom a lifelong interest in Asia was sparked by reading Abdullah.

A few swallows do not, of course, make a summer. But, as Jamie Mackie writes in his essay "Australian Creative Writers and Asia",[7] their appearance may indicate that a long winter is ending. During that winter, as Alison Broinowski indicates in her book *The Yellow Lady*, stock themes tediously recurred in Australian novels whose characters encounter Asia: the shock of arrival, the descriptions of smells, crowds and colours, the appearance of a local guide or mentor, the inevitable quest that provides a plot usually involving a journey into the interior or a climb to a mountain top, from which would arise enlightenment of some sort. Other clichés included, of course, the required transitory love affair with a foreign woman and, finally, departure for home. Broinowski wickedly pinpoints the case of Helen Heney's novel *The Chinese Camellia*,[8] in which the Australian hero "faced with the wellknown Western dilemma of how to cope with an Asian lover, eventually resolves it by the unusual means of sailing with Ch'a Fa to the Antarctic Ocean and there drowning her".

There are still some major obstacles in the way, one of which is the fact that a sorry tradition of racist and cultural stereotyping has left its stain on Australian thinking, and consequently on Australian writers and readers. Alison Broinowski lists Australian literary interpretations of Asia over the years that make discouraging reading. Here are a few examples.

1890s	As prosperity waned, Australian writers developed an obsession with skin colour. Novels called *The Yellow Wave*,[9] *Yellow and White*,[10] *The Yellow Man*[11] and *White or Yellow?*[12] glutted the market.
1895	The *Bulletin* saw Chinese and Japanese as equally threatening, but in 1895 it was somewhat confused about their colour: "The little brown men come leaping over our north-eastern and north-western border by scores and hundreds". The colour change to brown was necessary because they were being compared to a plague of rabbits.[13]
1896	Joseph Furphy used the expression "yellow" and "Yellow Agony" liberally in his novel *Such is Life*.[14]
1903	"Invasion fiction" was as popular, says Alison Broinowski, with Victorian Australians as science fiction is today.[15] Aldridge Evelyn, novelist, wrote of invasions of Australia "by every Chink and Jap under the sun", in *The Coloured Conquest*.[16]
1909	Louis Esson, nationalist playwright, after a visit to Japan and other countries, wrote a series of articles on the "Asiatic menace" and the "many dangers for the white race of the Pacific" for *The Lone Hand*:[17] "I feel sure Australia must be kept white, and have severe immigration laws... We'll have to find out what races will blend and prohibit all the rest."
1910	Jo Smith's play *The Girl of the Never Never*.[18] Its stage directions called for "a turbulent stream of yellow water rushing towards the footlights". Australia, says the hero of this play, must not become piebald: "We're going to keep this country, and we're going to keep it white".
1911	In Edmund Duggan's play, *My Mate*,[19] a bush drama sympathetic to Aborigines, the hero nonetheless announces that if he had his way, he'd give "the coloured races" 24 hours to get out.
1922	The poet Hugh McCrae and the artist and author Norman Lindsay jointly produced their poem *The Yellow Lady*.[20] The

writer Jack Lindsay (Norman's son) felt that "Of all the mass imbecilities which have demoralised mankind, this of racial equality between peoples, white, black, red and yellow, is the most inane".

1929   Edward Dyson referred collectively to the Chinese in his ballad "A Golden Shanty"[21] as "Celestials" and "The Yellow Agony".

1934   Ion Idriess wrote a collection of short stories called *The Yellow Joss*,[22] with a theme of race.

1942   T Stewart's novel *Yellow Spies*[23] was published.

Skin colour remained the underlying criterion for immigration, and hence for images of Asians in Australia until the late 1960s. In 1945, Australia's first Minister for Immigration, AA Calwell, summed it up when he said: "We have 25 years at most to populate this country before the yellow races are down on us".[24]

So one asks: How does the Australian writer cope with the subject of Asians in Australia? As poorly as he or she coped with that other manifestation of the "other", the subject of Aborigines in Australia. Works such as Mary Durack's *Kings in Grass Castles*[25] offer a sub-text which undermines the superficial courtesies of the colonial encounter: the British grazier, entering into the seeming emptiness of the Kimberleys, a region he clearly regards as his rightful inheritance, names the native inhabitants of the land after the vegetables and fruit that are a staple of the settler's table. The reader of Australian history may well see here a foreshadowing of a future, not very far away, in which British settlers in a new country, growing impatient with the Aboriginal people they found living on the land they desired to annex for their cattle-stations and grain-fields, consumed their lives, their prosperity and their ancient customs like so many dishes at a feast.

So one asks again — How does the Australian writer today cope with the subject of Asians in Australia? Considering the fact that there has been a Chinese presence in Australia since the Gold Rush and before, it is surprising that there has been little attempt to represent Asian Australians in fiction until quite recently. When I began in 1989 to write a novel that involved Asians living in

Australia, I could find no precedent or model to work from, no "tradition", however stereotypical, to link my own inventions to, except Barbara Baynton's story "Billy Skywonkie", in which an educated and cultured woman, brought into the bush as housekeeper and defacto partner for a selector, turns out to be part Chinese in origin, ie, Eurasian. As a result she has to face rejection and insult at the hands of persons (bushmen) who have been shown already, in their attitude to women of their own race, to be contemptible.

I see much of contemporary Australian writing about Asia (or set in Asia) as being more about Australians finding themselves than about Australians discovering Asia. Many contributors to this book focus on Australia's problems in coming to terms with her own identity by looking at Australia's relationships with Asia. As a writer, it has meant a lot to me. It would mean a lot to any writer who is attempting to define an Australian identity by placing it in the context of Asia.

India, however, has always been rather remote from Australia and the Australian writer. An academic colleague with interests in philosophy told me once that, despite the fascination Indian intellectual and spiritual explorations have for him, he has never been able to take really seriously a religion that takes a cow as its most sacred symbol. I thought at the time that he must be joking. Maybe it was a joke of the same kind as that other famous one which tells us *Hamlet* could never have been written in Australia, where the only dilemma facing the Prince could have been "To beer or not to beer". And yet, from time to time, I come across fascinating evidence that India, even mystic India, is not so remote from the Australian literary imagination after all. When I was working on my first novel, the Eleanor Dark Foundation provided me with every writer's dream: three weeks of perfect peace and quiet in which to complete the book. Eleanor Dark's house in Katoomba in the Blue Mountains is a large and comfortable house in what I take to be the Australian style of the 1930s. How surprising, then, to find that she and her husband Eric had named it "Varuna". Varuna is the name of a Hindu deity, a powerful personage with special control of clouds and seasons — just the right kind of muse, I feel, to invite into a writer's personal space.

We are now in an era of change, and the East is a-calling in tones very different from those that Kipling heard. Sources of information about the cultures and literatures of Asia are available now as they have never been before, and they say more about Asia than that it offers promising markets for Australian products. Let me identify some of those sources:

1. The lively English translations that are now becoming available of old and contemporary Asian texts.
2. A special broadcasting service in SBS that makes films made in Asia accessible to the Australian viewer.
3. Imaginative television versions of seminal Asian works, such as Roger Brook's *Mahabharatan*;[26]
4. Education about Asia presented in Australian schools and universities, a cause to which I am heavily committed.
5. Informed Australian reviewing of books by writers from Asia, by Asians writing in Australia.

Until fairly recently few critics and reviewers (apart from academics working in the area of "Asian Studies") possessed the kind of grounding in literature originating outside the West which could help them respond sensitively to writers who chose to use techniques and forms deriving from Asian literature, ancient and modern. This is certainly not the case today. There are writers of Asian origin whose fictional writing set in Australia and employing techniques drawn from both East and West have met appreciative and intelligent reviews here as well as overseas. Brian Castro is one such writer, and I include myself. As a published poet and fiction writer who abstained from seeking publication in Australia for 20 years in the belief, indeed the *knowledge,* that I was unlikely to find readers here, I find it very encouraging to be part of a culture that seems at long last to be developing its own distinctive literary identity; and to find that an intelligent understanding of Asia is part of that identity.

Some Thoughts on Asian Studies, Universities and the Teaching of Literature

Pierre Ryckmans

I have strong misgivings regarding the very concept of "Asian studies". The basic problem is, of course, the fact that *Asia does not exist*. "Asia" is a purely Western notion, an arbitrary fabrication; it has little or no basis in geography, culture and history. It is merely a legacy from the late imperialist-colonial era: it was then used as a convenient label to cover all-that-was-not-European, east of Europe; otherwise, it conveys no meaningful content. If one adopts a negative criterion, one can always lump together the most heterogeneous objects, and form incoherent and absurd collections. This fallacy is familiar to logicians: neither a goldfish, nor a bicycle, nor your grandmother is propelled by a steam-engine: this common negative feature does not create a specific category which should comprise all three. Similarly, the fact that, let us say, neither Japan nor Bangladesh belong to Western culture does not establish a meaningful link between the two, that would make it beneficial, or merely sensible, to attempt to study them jointly. Asia is hardly more than a Western prejudice, and the sooner we realise that there is a greater cultural distance between China and India, than between either one and

Europe, the better chance we might have eventually to reach a certain degree of understanding of these widely different worlds.

The whole issue of whether Australia might merge into Asia, or whether it might fail to do so is splendidly irrelevant. How can you endeavour to join — or abstain from joining — an entity that has no existence? The question would arise only if Asia was a monolith — but it is only a figment of European imagination, and in this sense, as diverse and evanescent as a rainbow.

Recently, a university which was putting its Faculty of Asian Studies under review (the exact aim of these periodic and costly exercises always remained an impenetrable mystery for me) invited me to contribute a submission, and suggested a long series of questions which my contribution should address. What struck me is that the only question that should really matter was absent from that list.

CS Lewis observed that, to assess the value of anything — be it a cathedral or a corkscrew — one should first know its purpose. What indeed should be the purpose of an Asian Studies Faculty — or of a university for that matter? Is it to *train* interpreters, marketing-consultants and travelling salesmen, in order "to serve the national interest"? Or is it *to educate* civilised minds by opening them to the Chinese, Japanese or Indian humanities? There are weighty arguments that could support either of these two options, but we should always bear in mind that they represent two totally different orientations. You cannot both devote yourself to teaching — let us say — Tang poetry and Song painting, *and* expect to be therefore performing a useful socio-politico-economic role for the national community. If we persist in confusing these two pursuits, the risk is that we shall fail on both grounds: on the one hand, we will not appreciate Tang poetry and Song painting — and on the other, we will not open any Asian markets.

This basic confusion is at the root of the crisis which now affects our entire Higher Education system. The problem was well illustrated by an intriguing phenomenon which took place during the past 20 years: in a first stage, "Colleges of Advanced Education" were established everywhere in the country to teach applied disciplines and to dispense the sort of practical vocational training that universities could not, and *should not* provide, since by their very definition, universities must exclusively devote themselves to *liberal* studies (in the sense which Newman ascribed to the concept: "that alone is *liberal* knowledge which stands on its own pretensions, which is independent of sequel, refuses to be informed by any end"[1]). Then, in a second stage, we saw a bizarre evolution taking place: these two streams — professional training on the one side, and liberal education on the other — which were originally meant to develop separately, began to merge, and today their confusion is complete. To consecrate this glorious muddle, the Colleges are now usurping all the titles and trappings that were supposed to be the exclusive preserve of the universities, whereas the universities make pathetic and clumsy efforts to discharge all the tasks that were better performed by the Colleges.

The consequences for the universities are disastrous, and the situation is going from bad to desperate. Are there any remedies? I can think of only two measures — simple and radical. Don't blame me for being utopian: in a terminal illness, utopian dreaming remains the ultimate medicine. First — universities should award no more degrees. Second — the intake of students should be cut by nine tenths.

Once degrees can no more be obtained from universities, a great illusion will be dispelled: it will become clear to all that, in practical terms, a university education *leads nowhere*. Implementation of my first suggestion will go a long way towards achieving my second proposal: people who originally wished to enter universities for the wrong reasons will naturally address themselves elsewhere; once they realise that no university can directly help them to secure an employment, they will turn towards vocational training institutions which are precisely geared towards that purpose. Universities will get much smaller numbers of applicants, — who will be mostly the right candidates. (And if further screening of applicants was still required, a basic *literacy* test at the entrance should at last ensure a drastic reduction of the usual intake of students.)

In the seventies, when there was some unrest on campus, I remember a most ludicrous slogan which "revolutionary" students had daubed on the walls of the university library: "Down with academic elitism!". Had they written: "Down with universities" and burnt the place, one could at least have appreciated a certain consistency in their position. If you do not want elitism, by all means get rid of universities — but I do not see how you could have the latter without the former.

University is elitist by very definition. Bertrand Russell observed: "University education should be regarded as a privilege for special ability".[2] Naturally he pursued: "Those who possess the skill but no money should be maintained at the public expense during their course". (To which we should also add: those who possess money but not the skill should be ruthlessly discouraged.)

When I claim that universities should be elitist, do not misunderstand my position and imagine that I am being antidemocratic. On the contrary, I am the staunchest partisan of democracy — in its proper sphere of application, which should be strictly limited to the socio-political area. In the socio-political area, nothing but democratic rules and principles will do. *Outside* the socio-political area, however, democratic principles have no relevance whatsoever: love is not democratic; beauty is not democratic; truth is not democratic; genius is not democratic. Let us invoke once more the old example of sport: in a country where people are always so wary of elitism in any line of activity, it is naturally accepted, cultivated and admired in sport. People who would object to more demanding criteria of entry into university would never dream to lower the standards of selection for the athletes we send to the Olympic Games!

Finally, on my third theme — the teaching of literature — allow me simply to quote here what I replied to an inquiry from the Higher Education Supplement of the *Australian*, at the conclusion of a lengthy debate on the use and purpose of academic literary theory:

Let us not kid ourselves: the study of literature is of no practical use whatsoever — unless one would wish to become, of all things, a professor of literature. This wise observation was made by Nabokov, I think, and we should keep it in mind when we try to understand the rich intricacies of contemporary literary theory.

Critics and literary scholars are merely the ushers of literature. In the concert hall, at the theatre or at the opera, ushers who take us to our seats perform a modest, yet useful, role. Actually they are useful only as long as they remain modest. Should the ushers suddenly insist on climbing on stage to sing and act alongside the artists we came to applaud, we might rightly resent their impertinence.

Literary criticism (not literary theory) presents a lasting value and deserves to be taken seriously only when it is produced by creative writers and when it constitutes itself a work of art.

EM Forster observed: "Study has a very solemn sound. 'I am studying Dante' sounds much more than 'I am reading Dante'. It is really much less. Study is only a serious form of gossip".[3]

For us, humble teachers, scholars and critics, the loftiest ambition, the highest achievement and the greatest source of pride will always remain this: to be able to stimulate in our audience a love for literature,* and to make them discover good and beautiful books.

---

*   The best teacher is not the one who loves his students, but the one who loves his subject.

COMMENTARY

CHILDREN'S LITERATURE AND IDENTITY

Q

What role does children's literature play in the progression of developing our Australian identity? In Australia, this genre has only recently moved away from English and, to a lesser extent, American images.

Yasmine Gooneratne

I had the kind of grounding probably that most Australians had — Beatrix Potter, *Alice in Wonderland*... I can tell you about the Flopsy Bunnies and their passion for soporific lettuce and so on. But I was lucky enough to have a couple of parents who were wonderful about buying books and among the books they bought us were the myths of Greece and Rome and the myths and legends of India. I came to Japanese and Chinese texts later. As a child I was perfectly free to roam where I wished in the bookshelves.

There is no distinction between children's and adults' literature in Asia. And also in the story-telling sessions which are still current in many parts of Asia, there is no feeling that the children should be sent away, as we normally do with television programs. Grey beards and little children all sit together hearing the most terrifying stories... princes and princesses who wander in forests and the princess gets pregnant... the farmer's wife who is unfaithful to the farmer and how the farmer manages to deal with this situation... So maybe the children are getting sex education early.

When it comes to children's literature, I am all for the idea of children being exposed to the literature of as many cultures as possible, particularly through the folk, because we are losing our contact with the natural sources of storytelling. We depend so much now on books, television and radio. So we really should try to get back to some of those sources and try to make sure the children's imagination grows. The more educators open up children's minds to literature that comes from different parts of the world the better — particularly beautifully illustrated literature which really takes the imagination. That is the most marvellous thing you can do for the growing literature of a country.

INDIGENOUS PEOPLE

Q

As this is the year of the indigenous, could you give us your thoughts on this matter?

Pierre Ryckmans

I confess I never gave much thought to the question (and I wish someone could show me why I should). The only relevant consideration (it seems to me) is that *we are all indigenous* on this common planet of ours. Beyond that, I am wary of the concept of indigeneity — perhaps, because I come from Europe. In continental Europe, except for tiny pockets of Celts and Basques in extreme western corners of the continent, there are no real indigenous nations: everyone displaced someone else, no one is occupying his rightful place. From this point of view, to promote "indegeneity" would be now a sure recipe for murderous chaos.

VII

AUSTRALIAN ARTISTS AND ASIA

INTRODUCTION

Marie Bashir

The arts, by way of expressing our dreams, our fantasies, our ideals, our agonies, our histories and our hopes for the future, are probably the most integrating and enduring aspects of any cultural identity. Indeed my own involvement with the South-East Asian refugee communities of Sydney began through the medium of art, when shortly after the first boat people arrived in New South Wales for resettlement, a worried school counsellor brought me a bundle of the children's drawings and paintings. The memories and experiences which were far too overwhelming for these youngsters to express even in the language of their country of origin are recorded in most eloquent and poignant art. They depicted epic journeys which they were only able to speak of much much later and which reminded me of Homer describing Troy's agony: "Even the stones would weep".

Since those early days, little more than a decade ago, we have seen an extraordinary proliferation of Asian cultural streams in our art, literature, music and theatre, and we know much more is to come. Increasing numbers of Australian artists are living and working in Asia, integrating these two streams of western and eastern art. Jacqueline Menzies has a deep interest in the arts of northern Asia, and in cross-cultural streams and exchanges amongst the artists of the many countries involved.

From Orientalism to Interchange Australian Artists to Asia 1870s-1990s

Jacqueline Menzies

No more clearly is a nation's self-identity articulated than through the images created by its artists. Literature, theatre and music can shape a culture, but it is the artists' images that remain as the immutable icons by which a nation distinguishes and transmits its cultural difference.

Australia's growing nationalism can be traced through images: the development of the Australian school of landscape painting through the efforts of Tom Roberts, Arthur Streeton and Charles Conder, who sought to establish a distinctly Australian art; and the subsequent creation of archetypal images of Australians by Russell Drysdale, William Dobell and Sidney Nolan (who, in his Ned Kelly series, distilled the ethos of white Australia's mythology).

Similarly Australia's evolving perceptions of Asia can be traced through the images of its artists. Perception is culturally determined; every now and then a talented individual attains an intuitive creative leap that re-aligns our way of seeing, in exactly the same way as an intellectual or scientist can change our way of thinking. So too the images of Asia produced by different Australian artists from the 1870s to the 1990s reflect shifting perceptions, as well as our growing independence from assumed European attitudes to self-reliant assessment and critical interchange. From our growing integration with Asia, I predict the emergence of new icons of national identity.

There were, of course, Australian artists who painted "oriental" scenes, worked in an "oriental" style or depicted Asian communities in Australia, without ever visiting Asia. This chapter concentrates on those artists who have visited an Asian country and the images they created.

The approach here is chronological, demonstrating most cogently the evolution of our images from ones framed by British perceptions to ones based on an independent maturity derived from the unique reality that underlies the contemporary experience of most Australians with Asia. The conclusion is that increasingly our evolving cultural identity includes an Asian component because the impact Asia exerts on us, as individuals and as a community — through trade, cuisine, personal relationships — is so woven through the fabric of our society as to have been absorbed without too much debate.

This chapter is split into the several sections that correspond with what I see as the distinguishing stages in our evolving cognisance of Asia as a series of distinct geographical places, each with its singular cultural heritage. The first of these sections I have termed Australian Orientalism. It covers the period from the 1870s, when Asia was perceived as the Oriental "other", through to the outbreak of World War I. By the 1870s a colonial identity had been established in Australia, there was the wealth to travel, establish art schools and even a local art community.

I have used the term Australian Orientalism to incorporate the colonial versions of the two 19th century European movements relating to the perception of Asia: Orientalism (dealing with the Middle and Near East — near to Europe not Australia, ie countries like Turkey) and Japonisme, the term that refers to the impact of Japanese art and aesthetics on the European consciousness. In Europe, the Orient was less a place, or places, of geographical definition, than part of a Western discourse with the exotic "other".

The next section covers the fashionable 1920s and the period between the two world wars. The post-war period I have divided into the decades 1950s to 1970s; and the 1970s to 1990s. The latter period saw a major shift in our cultural relationship to Asia for a variety of complex reasons. Firstly the influx of refugees and immigrants resulting from the Vietnam War, then the establishment of diplomatic relations with the Peoples Republic of China, together with a growing cultural maturity, symbolised by the establishment of the Australia Council in 1973. Since that crucial decade there has been an important realignment in our cultural aspirations, which is the concluding section of this chapter.

Given the early tainted association of Australia with the belief it was the Antipodes, the opposite to the norm, it is perhaps not surprising that early artists sought recognition at the centre of the Empire by adopting fashionable English painting styles and aspiring to be exhibited at the Royal Academy in London. As far as Asia was concerned, the lure for Australian painters and travellers was that of their English and European mentors: the sensory experience of the exotic "Oriental" countries of the Middle East. From the end of the 18th century to World War I, the North African states of Morocco, Algeria and Tunisia, as well as Egypt, the Holy Land, Syria, Lebanon and Turkey, epitomised the exotic other, the lands of harems, sultans and minarets, immortalised through the Romantic literature of Byron and poems such as Coleridge's "Kubla Khan" (1816). The experience of the Orient was facilitated for many when Thomas Cook established tours to Egypt in 1868.

In London, Frederic Lord Leighton, the great 19th century classical painter and President of the Royal Academy, the epitome of the cultivated artist Australian artists aspired to be, extended his home Leighton House in 1877-79 to create the centrepiece, the Arab Hall, an architectural folly lined with Islamic tiles.

European artists reserved a highly detailed, naturalistic style of painting for their depictions of the rich, sensual world of the mysterious East. Such Orientalist paintings were the visual manifestation of Orientalism, the special Western construct for dealing with the "other" so critically analysed by Edward Said in his book *Orientalism*.[1] Now regarded as icons of European colonial expansion, aspirations and fantasies, Orientalist paintings in their day justified European dominance of their Eastern colonies. Colonial artists, aspiring not just to be part of the British Empire, but for recognition at the centre as represented by the Royal Academy, perpetuated this tradition.

A respected colonial artist who gained recognition in London for his Orientalist pictures was Robert Dowling (1827-86). Dowling, brought up in Tasmania, went to London in his late twenties, visited Cairo in 1872-73, and subsequently had his magnificent 1874 painting "A Sheikh and his son entering Cairo on their return from Mecca" exhibited at the Royal Academy in 1875 and purchased by the National Gallery of Victoria in 1878, where it was displayed as proud proof of the colonial son's success.

Australian artists' experience of "Asia" in the late 19th to early 20th century focussed on the "Orient" conceptualised by Europe and depicted it through the Oriental framework. On their voyage to London (and Paris), the great rite of passage for the colonies' cultural elite, they would stop at Colombo and visit Cairo and Luxor as a break from shipboard life. From the opening of the Suez Canal in 1869, for nearly a century, this was the experience of the Orient for many Australians.[2] The Asia they saw was only that which they passed on their way to Europe or visited because of its exoticism.

Roberts, Conder and Streeton all made the trip to this Orient, painting light-filled rhapsodies to the Moorish architecture and the exotically garbed but anonymous people. Charles Conder (1868-1909) visited Algiers in 1891, one year after leaving Australia, to recuperate from the excesses which would eventually destroy him and to experience in reality a place of his fantasies, the land of the Arabian nights. There he painted the haunting, melancholic *Flowers in a vase against a background of the coast of Mustapha* (on permanent display in the Art Gallery of New South Wales), an enigmatic work tinged with unexpressed fears, a far more potent and personal statement than most Orientalist pictures.

Streeton wrote of his visit to Cairo, of which there are several extant watercolours: "'Tis a wonderful land this Egypt; I've been time after time through the slipper, brass and bronze, jewellery, perfume, silks, ring, curio bazaars — and yesterday with another artist I did a quick sketch of a spice bazaar; and the alley was choc-a-block all the time — hundreds of Arabs standing round...with many a grand old face..."[3]

Emmanuel and Ethel Carrick Fox visited North Africa in 1911, painting in Morocco, Algeria and Spain. Ethel returned again to North Africa in the early 1920s. Although born and educated in London, and only resident in Australia intermittently through her life, Ethel is regarded as an Australian artist. Another female artist who enjoyed the brilliant colour and light of North Africa was Hilda Rix Nicolas, who visited Tangier in 1912 and again in 1914. Both she and Ethel Carrick painted colourful market places, that focussed on overall ambience and were devoid of unpleasant sights or anything Western.

For most Australians, the adopted European view of Egypt as the gateway to the Orient was dramatically changed with the advent of World War I when our troops were exposed to the reality of war, the sun and sand of Egypt, and the explosion of the Oriental myth.

If Lord Leighton's Arab room had epitomised the craze for Islamic cultures, Whistler's Peacock room was the penultimate expression in architectural terms of the simulation of the decorative beauty of Japanese art. Japanese art had begun to seriously influence French artists from the 1860s when the bold compositions, bright flat colours and original perspectives of Japanese prints were a revelation. From that time, the impact of Japanese arts rippled through the fine and decorative art traditions of the West, creating the movement known as Japonisme, the basic tenets of which were the foundations of Art Nouveau and Aestheticism.

Aestheticism in Australia flourished from the 1870s when Japanese goods were seen in huge numbers in various intercolonial and International exhibitions (eg Sydney 1879; Melbourne 1880). The craze for Japanese goods shaped the taste of middle-class interiors; while Roberts, Streeton, and Conder, in absorbing the principles of Japanese painting, were "not at all free from the charge of Whistlerism".[4]

The impact of Japanese art, albeit mediated through English examples, on Australian consciousness generated an interest in Japan that resulted in several influential artists visiting the country. In the

1870s EL Montefiore (1820-94), an etcher and the first director of the Art Gallery of New South Wales, visited Japan, while the architect John Smedley practised for some years in Yokohama. In 1887 and 1896, Mortimer Mempes (1859-1938), expatriate follower of Whistler, visited Japan, subsequently producing numerous paintings, prints and books.

The vogue for Japanese art continued well into the early 20th century, fuelled internationally by a resurgence of interest in the woodcut, of which the Japanese were the quintessential masters. Australian artists, still emulating the practices of the London art world, studied F Morley Fletcher's 1916 book[5] on woodblock printing in the Japanese method, and stylistically were influenced not only by traditional ukiyo-e prints, but also by contemporaneous Japanese prints which were part of an international vogue for the new modern woodcut. This vogue was reflected in the publications of two special issues of the *Studio*: "Modern Woodcuts and Lithographs" (1919) and "The New Woodcut" (1930).

An artist responsive to this vogue who decided to visit Japan itself was Paul Haefliger, a cosmopolitan man of catholic tastes, a collector, connoisseur and art critic for the *Sydney Morning Herald* from 1942 to 1957. He visited Japan in 1932, specifically to study the art of the colour woodcut, and his few extant landscape prints reflect the influence of Hiroshige.

Margaret Preston toured Japan in 1934, creating images of bunraku puppets to accompany her article "The puppet theatre of Osaka, Japan" in Manuscripts, February 1935. Preston also collected several illustrated books in Japan, the annotated pages of which attest to the impact of their designs on her own work. Likewise her own much-used copy of Ernest Fenollosa's influential book *Epochs of Chinese and Japanese Art*[6] reinforces the importance of Asian art to her own work. Preston also visited Peking and Korea.

Throughout the inter-war period, Japanese art, specifically prints and decorative arts (not so much the paintings esteemed by the Japanese themselves to which there was little Western exposure), was associated with the modern and the fashionable. Likewise with Chinese art, particularly after the 1935 International Exhibition of

Chinese Art in London. No fashionable interior in Sydney was without its Chinese or Japanese accessories.

In terms of tracing the development of Australia's cultural involvement with Asia, this period marked one step closer to a better understanding. Exposure to those countries' art, specifically that of China and Japan, fostered an interest that led to travel. Throughout the 1920s and 1930s it was extremely fashionable to take a cruise to the "Far East", as well as the traditional one through the Suez Canal on the way "home".

The prints created by artists such as Preston, shaped by exposure to authentic examples of Asian art, was not as prescribed an interpretation as the earlier Australian Orientalist paintings, which reflected a Western construct, and which never acknowledged in any way whatsoever the artistic conventions of the countries depicted.

The first influential artist to visit Asia had in fact been the architect Hardy Wilson, who spent three months in China in 1922. When he returned, he exhibited his collection at the Art Gallery of New South Wales, including a silk painting of a phoenix which was the model for the bird that appears in many of his architectural drawings. Wilson developed his idea of uniting East and West, a theme he was to reiterate constantly in his writings, his architectural drawings and even his designs for furniture. He was the first Australian of influence to envisage the fusion of Australia's western heritage with our experience of Asia. His vision of Australia's unique future was encapsulated in his cover design for his book *Atomic Civilization*,[7] 1949: a lyre bird, the symbol of Australia, standing midway between the phoenix, symbol of the east, and the hawk, symbol of the west (America). (Interestingly, a version of this idea was expressed later by composer Peggy Glanville-Hicks, a keen advocate of Indian music, who saw the triangle in terms of the new English-speaking countries — India, Australia and America[8]).

Artists such as Wilson and Preston were exceptional in their premonition of Australia's closer involvement with Asia. Certainly for most people at the time, artists included, England and Europe were still the centre of a world where we occupied the periphery. The news in our papers was European news; we had no Department of External Affairs of our own until 1936; and Asia, with the exception of a worrying Japan and a turbulent China, was subject to the colonial rule of Britain, the Netherlands, France and the United States.[9]

This situation was drastically and permanently changed with World War II, the conclusion of which led, amongst many things, to independence for India and Pakistan (1947), Indonesia (1949) and Malaya (1957).

Although the trauma and disaster of the war was a schism through the century, it had strangely little impact on our "high" culture. The 1940s wars in Malaya, Burma and Thailand, and the later war in Vietnam left little response in the work of Australian painters. Rather, personal responses were expressed through magazine illustrations, cartoons, films and such more immediate and accessible popular art forms.

Of the several artists who received official War Artist Commissions and were posted to parts of Asia — for example Murray Griffin, Sali Herman and Eric Thake — any work they did in Asia related more to the idea of war than the experience of Asia.

One artist who served in the army for a desperately unhappy period between 1942 and 1946 was Donald Friend. While still a boy, Friend had dreamed of the exotic, first visiting Africa before the war. After the war he visited Italy and then he had an artistically fruitful four years in Colombo. In 1966 he moved to Bali, where he stayed more or less continuously for the next 13 years, with his life in Bali becoming a legend in Australia. Donald immersed himself in Balinese culture, revelling in the relaxed lifestyle of a South Seas paradise that had been luring European globetrotters since the 1930s, collecting Balinese art, and infusing his paintings with Balinese motifs and pictorial conventions.

Another restless artist who lived in Asia was Ian Fairweather, whose first experience of China, its landscape and the magnificent calligraphy of its masters, was to constantly inspire his creativity. Fairweather first visited Australia in 1934, then returned to China and travelled to various other Asia destinations before settling in Bribie Island. Together with Friend, he represents a further shift in the relationship of Australian artists to Asia: both rejected their own culture and chose to live in an Asian one and assimilate the lessons of its painting into their own idiosyncratic statement. Their work marks another stage from the mainly technique-based interest of the printmakers.

While most of the interaction between Australian artists and Asia concerns painters, an important potter whose travels in China sparked his own interests was Ivan McMeekin. In 1946 McMeekin signed a three-year contract with the China Navigation Company, and was exposed to the great traditions of Chinese and Korean ceramics. He went on to study in England with Michael Cardew, a former pupil of Bernard Leach, the acknowledged leader of the modern folk art pottery movement. These traditions McMeekin introduced into Australia through his teaching, and in 1967 published his influential handbook *Notes for Potters in Australia*[10] which, amongst other things, instructed potters on the use of local clays.

For most artists however, America was now the drawcard. England, as the centre of the Commonwealth, was still influential for the community at large: Asia was still a Commonwealth Asia rather than a geographic Asia, a concept reinforced by programs such as the Colombo plan, which were instrumental in breaking down barriers and laying the foundations of individual networks.

In the 1960s Japan became a noticeable influence on Australian culture. The 1960s was a period of social change, experimentation, hippies, the Beatles and meditation. Abstract expressionism, Zen, improvisation and Pop were all part of the melange of concepts and movements endorsed at that time. The hippie revolution was global, but in Australia it did mean many young Australians became familiar with local Asian cultures as they embarked on the "overland travel" to northern India, Nepal and Europe.

The artistic climate of 1960s in Sydney was epitomised by *The Yellow House* in Potts Point in which young artists mounted innovative displays. For example, Brett Whiteley organised a "Bonsai Show" in 1971 and invited various artists to submit their representation of a bonsai. Whiteley maintained an interest in Eastern philosophies and calligraphy throughout his life.

An artist absorbed in calligraphy was Royston Harpur, who spent 1972 in Kyoto studying calligraphy. His work was exhibited with that of Whiteley, Peter Upward, and several potters in an exhibition entitled "The Calligraphic Image" at the Art Gallery of New South Wales. This was the first exhibition to acknowledge the spreading impact of Asian aesthetics and ideas on contemporary Australian artists. The work of potters such as Peter Rushforth, Milton Moon and others who had worked in Japan was included. Through the influence of the Bernard Leach/Shoji Hamada philosophy, there was much exchange between Australia and Japan. Most of the influence was Japan-centred because Japan, as a result of its familiarity with Western institutions, the American occupation, and its strengthening economy, was the Asian country with the highest profile in the West. Although formal diplomatic relations with the Peoples Republic of China were established in 1972, the Cultural Revolution persisted until 1976, and the gradual development of individual exchanges was truncated with the Tiananmen Square incident of 1989.

From the 1970s, artists, along with other Australians, began to travel throughout their region, and to realise its importance to Australia. Major Australian artists praising Asia included John Olsen, Sidney Nolan (who exhibited a special series on China in 1990) and Fred Williams, who wrote in 1976 that "the only issue that is important for Australian art is to fight our pathetic isolation from our Asian neighbours".[11] Artists from neighbouring countries also visited, although mainly from Japan, and for special occasions such as the 1976 Biennale in Sydney, which had a large Japanese component.

The most recent period in the stages of our evolving relationship with Asia is what I have termed the "post-Vietnam period". The first Vietnamese boat people arrived in Australia in 1976. Some 51 vessels carrying 2001 people subsequently arrived, and ultimately Australia settled 37,000 refugees.[12] The community acceptance of the Indo-Chinese refugee outflow, and their acceptance of a higher immigration from non-Western countries generally, has had a major impact on Australian society. Sympathy for the repercussions of the recent incident of Tiananmen Square has also facilitated the quick acceptance of new Chinese immigrants.

The Garnaut report of 1990 published polls showing that 63 percent of the Australian community opted for giving higher priority to the Asia-Pacific rather than Europe (25 percent).[13] The report stressed the importance of cultural relations in developing the perceptions of a foreign society. Expanding cultural relations has been revealed in China as a cost-effective way of changing perceptions that are helpful to widening opportunities for productive exchange of many kinds.[14]

In 1983 the first exhibition of Australian contemporary art to travel to Asia was to Japan: the "Continuum '83" exhibition. The exhibition, which involved several artists going to Japan, was part of an exchange that started when several Japanese artists visited Melbourne in 1981 to participate in the exhibition "Yo-in — Ideas from Japan made in Australia". Artists in this show who have maintained a long and fulfilling relationship with Japan include Peter Callas, John Davis and Stelarc.

By the 1980s, the individual exchanges between artists, critics, art schools, and galleries, that had begun in the 1970s, was prolific. Multiculturalism and post-modernism both eased the acceptance and the promotion of exchanges from South, South-East and North Asia. Pluralism, diversity and regionalism were the catchwords, engendering a healthy confidence in one's own personal response as an individual from a specific background with a specific viewpoint. Euro-America was no longer seen as a centre of which Australia was at the perimeter. Now Australia was seen as a centre as valid as any other. Terence Maloon re-iterated this in his text for the "Continuum '83" catalogue: "The increasing dialogue and cultural exchanges with Asian and Pacific nations have the paramount importance of enabling Australians to understand their true geographic location, and to see their future as a Pacific, not a displaced European, nor a provincial Anglo-American, nation".

In 1990 in Melbourne, Asialink was formed as a joint initiative of the Myer Foundation, the Commission for the Future, and the Asian Studies Council, to promote understanding between Asia and Australia. Its mission statement is "to help create a new generation of Australians: people confident of living and working in partnerships with other countries of the Asian region. By the year 2000 it aims to create a more Asia-aware and Asia-literate Australia".

FROM ORIENTALISM TO INTERCHANGE

Each year Asialink funds six artists to spend four months working in Asia at one of the residencies they have established in the Philippines, Malaysia, Indonesia, Thailand and China. The program of supporting Australian artists and craftspeople to spend time in various Asian cities, attached to an art institution, had been begun by the Australia Council in 1988, but is now run by Asialink.

In 1991 the Australia Council (established 1973) announced it would increase the amount of its international budget allocated to the Asia/Pacific region from around 12 percent to 50 percent by 1992-93 — approximately $2 million.[15] The Councils' Chairman Rodney Hall explained that "there can be no doubt that Australia's future is essentially linked to Asia. This does not signal any attempted severance of our deep connections with Europe and America, simply the striking of a new balance".

The various government funding from different bodies now flowing into cultural exchange, has seen a huge increase in exchanges between individuals, as well as the increase of exhibitions of contemporary art touring Asian cities. These exchanges and exhibitions are too numerous to list but they are having an indelible impact on our artistic community. In 1990, Asialink's Alison Carroll curated the first exhibition to focus on contemporary Australian artists' views of Asia and its art.

Other examples of exchange and exhibitions between Australian artists and Asia include ones with Vietnam and Thailand. In the case of Vietnam, artists Rozalind Drummond and Geoff Lowe devised an exhibition of their work after visiting Vietnam in 1991. The exhibition works related to their own ongoing practice as artists, arising from their interchanges with their Vietnamese counterparts. Vietnam is important to Australia — as Lowe remarked, "Vietnam is part of our history, not as a place, but as an idea and a memory of a time".[16]

Another example of interchange was the exhibition "Thai-Australian Cultural Space", which was held at the Bangkok National Gallery in May 1993. This show involved the work of five installation artists — two Australians, Joan Grounds and Noelene Lucas, and three Thais, Kamol Phaosavasdi, Montien Boonma and Vichoke Mukdamanee. All the artists had come to know and respect each other's work through institutional and personal contact in Australia and Thailand. While working in another country, each had been extended and their lives enriched in various ways that flowed through into their individual works. It is through such continuing interchanges that icons of a new Australia, radically different from earlier nationalist ones, will emerge to become enmeshed in our image of ourselves in the 21st century.

There is finally one aspect of Australian artists going to Asia that I have not mentioned, and that is Australian-Asian artists returning to an Asian country, or perhaps, in the case of an Australian-born Chinese (an "ABC" in popular language) visiting China for the first time, perhaps through the impetus of multiculturism.

If just the Chinese are considered, Australia has had a long involvement with Chinese immigrants, from the 19th century days of the gold rush, to the most recent arrivals. Many of the early Australian reactions to the Chinese have been graphically recorded through cartoons, revealing attitudes that embarrass and appal a modern reader.

However things have changed a lot for contemporary Chinese artists in Australia. This emerged quite strongly in a seminar held at the Art Gallery of New South Wales in June 1993. Entitled "Asian Voices", the all-day program was divided into three sessions entitled "Tradition and beyond", "Identity: the tyranny of appearance" and "Mainland Chinese voices". This seminar was the forum for artists of diverse Chinese backgrounds to articulate their feelings and experiences about being an artist in our contemporary society. Several points emerged such as the conflict of upbringing and education, and the question of a hybrid culture that emerges if you try to transplant one cultural form into a different environment. Another point was that for artists new to Australia, the dislocation from old cultures was a very intense experience because of the interaction of different cultures. Andrew Lo spoke about using Chinese traditional methods to paint the Australian bush — for him the Australian landscape has been interpreted by Aboriginal artists, European immigrant artists and now Asian migrant artists. So his message was the same as that of those other Australian artists involved in Asian interchanges: we are in the process of seeing a new

Australian visual vocabulary being created, out of which will emerge icons as potent and distinctive as Nolan's Ned Kelly.

ENDNOTES

I IDENTITY AND CHANGE

A National Movement that Includes Us All
— Thomas Keneally

1. See the letter of Ross in Colonial Office 201/2 Ed. See also Manning Clark: *History of Australia* Vol I, Melbourne University Press 1979, pp 74-90.
2. See also KG Allan, "Barron Field: his association with New South Wales", *Journal Royal Historical Society* Vol 53, 1967.
3. Barron Field, *First Fruits of Australian Poetry*, Sydney, 1819.
4. AD Hope, "Australia", *Collected Poems*, Angus & Robertson, 1966.
5. DH Lawrence, *Kangaroo*, 1923, Penguin edition in association with William Heinemann, 1954.
6. Ibid p 186.
7. Ibid p 187.
8. Ibid p 188.
9. Patrick White, *Voss*, Penguin Books, 1981.
10. D Campbell, "Night Sowing" *Selected Poems (1942-68)*, Angus & Robertson, 1968.
11. See generally, JA Le Nauze, *Alfred Deakin: A Biography*, Melbourne University Press, 1965.
12. See also Commonwealth Parliamentary Debates, 19 September 1922, Vol 100, pp 2347-2363.

II VOICES FROM MULTICULTURAL AUSTRALIA

Introduction
— Jeanette Beaumont

1. A Riemer, *Inside Outside: Life Between Two Worlds*, Imprint lives, Angus & Robertson, 1992.
2. A Riemer, *Habsburg Café*, 1993. Angus & Robertson, Imprint, 1993.
3. J Oppenheimer and B Mitchell, *An Australian Clan, The Nivisons of New England*, Kangaroo Press, 1989.

III THE CONSTITUTION

Introduction
— Margaret Beazley

1. *Commonwealth of Australia Constitution Act* 1900 63 & 64 Victoria Chapter 12.

ENDNOTES

Origins of the Australian Constitution
— Margaret Beazley

1. *Nelungaloo Pty Ltd v Commonwealth* (1952) 85 CLR 545 at 573

What the Constitution Says
— Sir Maurice Byers

1. *Western Australia v Chamberlain Industries Pty Ltd* (1970) 121 CLR 1 at 26-7.
2. *Victoria v Commonwealth* (1975) 134 CLR 338 at 404-6.
3. *Victoria v Commonwealth* (1975) 134 CLR 338 at 396-8.
4. *Judiciary Act* 1903 (Cth) ss 38 and 39.
5. *Fencott v Muller* (1983) 152 CLR 570 at 609-610.
6. *Burns v Ransley* (1949) 79 CLR 1 and *R v Sharkey* (1949) 79 CLR 121
7. *Australian Communist Party v Commonwealth* (1951) 83 CLR 1 at 187-8; *Victoria v Commonwealth* (1975) 134 CLR 338 at 362, 397.
8. *Murphyores Incorporated Pty Ltd v Commonwealth* (1976) 136 CLR 1.
9. *Commonwealth v Tasmania* (1983) 158 CLR 1.
10. *R v Public Vehicles Licensing Appeal Tribunal* (1964) 113 CLR 207 at 225-6.

Is Change Recommended?
— Sir Maurice Byers and Sir Harry Gibbs

1. *HC Sleigh Ltd v South Australia* (1977) 136 CLR 475.
2. Quick and Garran, Commentary on the Constitution, at 837.
3. *Phillip Morris v Commissioner of Business Franchises (Vic)* (1989) 167 CLR 339.
4. *Philip Morris Ltd v Commissioner of Business Franchises (Vic)* (1984) 167 CLR 399 at p 425.
5. See, for example, *Commonwealth Oil Refineries Ltd v South Australia* (1926) 38 CLR 408 and *John Fairfax and Sons Ltd v New South Wales* (1926) 39 CLR 139.
6. *Dennis Hotels Pty Ltd v Victoria* (1960) 104 CLR 529; *Dickenson's Arcade Pty Ltd v Tasmania* (1974) 130 CLR 177; *Philip Morris Ltd v Commissioner of Business Franchises (Vic)*, supra.
7. *MG Kailis (1962) Pty Ltd v Western Australia* (1974) 130 CLR 245; *Gosford Meats Pty Ltd v New South Wales* (1985) 155 CLR 368.
8. *Western Australia v Hammersley Iron Pty Ltd (No 1)* (1969) 120 CLR 42; *Western Australia v Chamberlain Industries Pty Ltd* (1970) 121 CLR 1.
9. *Hematite Petroleum Pty Ltd v Victoria* (1983) 151 CLR 599.
10. *Rainsong Holdings Pty Ltd v ACT*, unreported; *Capital Duplicators (No 2) v ACT*, unreported.
11. *Victoria v Commonwealth* (1957) 99 CLR 575, at pp 606-7.
12. *Re F; Ex parte F* (1986) 161 CLR 377; *Cormick v Cormick* (1984) 156 CLR 177.
13. *Commonwealth v Tasmania (the Tasmanian Dam Case)* (1983) 158 CLR 1.
14. *Koowarta v Bjelke-Petersen* (1982) 153 CLR 168; and see *Queensland v Commonwealth* (1989) 167 CLR 232.
15. Quick and Garran at 704.
16. *Re Amendment of the Constitution of Canada* (1981) 1 SCR 753; 125 DLR (3d) 1.
17. *Brewer v Williams* (1977) 430 US 387.
18. *Nix v Williams* (1984) 81 Law Ed (2d) 377.
19. *MOT v Noort* [1992] 3 NZLR 260.

ENDNOTES

IV   BRAVE NEW REPUBLIC

Introduction
— Kim Santow

1. HG Wells, *The History of Mr Polly*, Macmillan, London, 1910.

Commentary
1. Sir John Kerr, *Matter for Judgment*, Macmillan, South Melbourne, 1978.
2. Sir Owen Dixon, "Sources of Legal Authority", *Jesting Pilot*, Law Book Co, 1965, pp 198-202. Also, per Dean J *Breavington v Godleman* (1988) 169 CLR 41 at 123.

V   IDENTIFYING WITH ASIA

An Australian Presence in Asia? An Australia Foundation?
— Alison Broinowski

1. A Broinowski, *The Yellow Lady*, Oxford University Press, Melbourne, 1992.

Australian-Asian Perceptions
— Anthony Milner

1. See "Issues in Citizenship", Deakin lecture, Sir Ninian Stephen, 1993, Melbourne Law Review [forthcoming].

VII   AUSTRALIAN AND ASIAN LITERATURE

Introduction
— Robin Marsden

1. S Leys, *Chinese Shadows*, New York, Viking, 1977.
2. S Leys, *Death of Napoleon*, London, Quartet Books, 1991, Sydney, Allen & Unwin, 1992.
3. Y Gooneratne, *A Change of Skies*, Sydney, Picador, 1991.

Asia in the Australian Literary Imagination
— Yasmine Gooneratne

1. Y Gooneratne, *Change of Skies* Sydney, Picador, 1991.
2. Ibid pp 11-12.
3. Lord JB Macauley, *The Great Minute on Indian Education*, The Supreme Council of India, 1835. See generally, Macauley's *Complete Works*, Albany Edition, 1898.
4. J Thomson, *The Seasons*, London, 1750. *Winter* appears in The Penguin Book of English Verse, 1980.
5. A Broinowski, *The Yellow Lady Australian Impressions of Asia*, Oxford University Press, Melbourne, 1992, p 14.

6. M Abdullah, *Time of the Peacock*, Angus & Robertson, 1992.
7. J Mackie, "Australian Creative Writers and Asia", 1992.
8. H Heney, *The Chinese Camellia*, Collins, Collins, London, 1950.
9. K Mackay, *The Yellow Wave: A Romance of the Asiatic Invasion of Australia*, Richard Bentley & Co, London, 1895.
10. C Dawe, *Yellow and White, Invasion of Australia*, London, 1895.
11. C Dawe, *The Yellow Man*, London, 1900.
12. W Lane, "White or Yellow? A Story of Race War in AD 1908", in *The Boomerarng*, 1888.
13. A Broinowski, *The Yellow Lady*, Oxford University Press, Melbourne, 1992, .p 11
14. J Furphy ("Tom Collins"), *Such is Life*, Angus & Robertson, Sydney 1945.
15. A Broinowski, *The Yellow Lady*, Oxford University Press, Melbourne, 1992, .p 11
16. A Evelyn, *The Coloured Conquest*, London, 1903.
17. L Esson, articles concerning the Asiatic Menace, in *The Lone Hand*, 1909.
18. J Smith, *The Girl of the Never Never*, 1910.
19. E Duggan, *My Mate*, 1911.
20. H McCrae, "The Yellow Lady", in *Idyllica*, Norman Lindsay Press, Sydney, 1922.
21. E Dyson, "The Golden Shanty", *Bulletin*, reappeared 1929.
22. I Idriess, *The Yellow Joss and other Tales*, Angus & Robertson, 1934.
23. WT Stewart, *Yellow Spies*, Currawong Publishing Co, Sydney, 1942.
24. See also AA Calwell, *How Many Australians Tomorrow?* Reed & Harris, Melbourne, 1945.
25. M Durack, *Kings in Grass Castles*, (1959) Lloyd O'Neil Pty Ltd, Melbourne, 1974.
26. [*Mahabharatan*, one of the two major Hindu epics.]

Some Thoughts on Asian Studies
— Pierre Ryckmans

1. JH Newman, *The Idea of a University*, ed IT Ker, Oxford, 1985.
2. B Russell, *On Education* Unwin Paperbacks, London 1976.
3. EM Forster, *Two Cheers for Democracy*, ("Anonymity: An Inquiry"), Penguin, Harmondsworth, 1972.

VIII AUSTRALIAN ARTISTS AND ASIA

From Orientalism to Interchange — Australian Artists to Asia 1870s-1990s
— Jacqueline Menzies

1. Vintage Books, New York, 1979.
2. R White, "Sun, Sand and Syphilis" in "Australian Perceptions of Asia", *Australian Cultural History*, No 9, 1990, p 50. White also states how Egypt and British control of the canal were seen as absolutely vital to Australia's commercial and strategic interests in much the same way that Asia is being reconstructed as vital to those interests today.
3. A Galbally, *Arthur Streeton*, Melbourne, Lansdowne, 1969, p 65.
4. A Galbally, "Aestheticism in Australia" in *Australian Art and Architecture*, Essays presented to Bernard Smith, edited by A Bradley and T Smith, Oxford, 1980, p 132.
5. F Morley Fletcher, *Wood-Block Printing Based on the Japanese Practice*, John Hogg, London, 1916.
6. William Heinemann, London, 1912.
7. Published by the author, printed by Ruskin Press, Melbourne, 1949.

ENDNOTES

8. A Broinowski, *The Yellow Lady*, Oxford University Press, Melbourne, 1992, p 94.
9. NSW University Press, Sydney, 1967.
10. J Legge, "Asian Studies, From Reconstruction to Deconstruction" in *Australian Cultural History*, No 9, 1990, p 94.
11. Quoted in "Continuum '83" catalogue, Japan-Australia Cultural and Art Exchange Committee, 1983.
12. P Luck, *Australian ICONS*, Melbourne, Heinemann, 1992, p 47.
13. R Garnaut, *Australia and the Northeast Asian Ascendancy*, Australian Government Publishing Service, 1990.
14. Ibid, p 332.
15. *Age*, 21 September 1991.
16. *Time*, April 5, 1993, in Asialink's Vietnam report.

INDEX

Aboriginals, 4, 28, 36, 42, 43, 98
    prejudice against, 29
    reconciliation with, 27
    treaty with, 27, 81
    see also Mabo
Adversarial
    legal system, 128
    two-party system, 21, 22
    see also Politics
Alienation, 6-8
Amnesty International, 164
Antipodes, 194
Arts, Australian and Asian, 191ff
Asia, 23, 113ff
    APEC, 146, 164, 165
    ASEAN, 113, 115, 119, 143, 144, 152, 164
    Asian Studies, 182ff
    Australian location in, 24
    Australian presence in, 115ff
    diplomatic and political ties with, 139ff
    economic productivity and, 41
    education of Asians, 118
    identifying with, 113ff
    national interest and, 120
    peoples, 42, 48
    perception of as monolithic, 117, 182-3, 195-6
    perceptions of Australia, 29, 122ff
    republic and, 107, 108
    see also Ethnic; Immigration; Literature; Multicultural; Multiracial; Arts
Asialink, 202, 203
Assimilation, 23
    see also Ethnic; Immigration; Multicultural
Australia Acts 1986, 59, 60, 87
    s 11, 64
Australia Foundation, 120-123
Australian-Asian Perceptions Project, 122ff
Bannon, Justice, 102
Barton, Edmond, 4, 9
Bill of Rights, 55, 75ff
    human rights and, 80
    see also Constitution; Judiciary
Black Australia, *see* Aboriginals
Bosnia 28
Bureaucrats, 80
    see also Executive power
Bush, 25, 35, 48-49
    see also Rural identity
Campbell, David, 8
Canada, 87, 88, 116
Central government power, *see* Commonwealth; States
Certainty, *see* Regulation
Children, *see* Marriage
China, 44, 129
Chinese art, 197, 198
    Australian artists and, 204
Citizenship, 124-125
    Australian, 23
    see also Migrants
Class, social structure, *see* Demographics; Egalitarianism; Redistribution
Colony, before Federation, 61
    see also Federation

INDEX

Commonwealth, 5, 61ff, 88
    Constitution and defined nature of powers conferred, 71
    external affairs, 71
    national economy and express Constitutional powers, 70, 71
    powers precedent over States where conflict, 71
    taxation powers, 67, 68
    treaty, power to negotiate, 81
    see also Constitution; Literature; Federation; Parliament; States

Compulsory voting and fixed terms, 103ff

Conder, Charles, 195

Constitution, 9, 10, 55ff, 85ff, 98ff, 102ff
    Australian people, and the, 60, 85
    British values and, 102
    change of, 67ff
    civil rights and, 27
    development of, 57
    families and, 70
    federal powers, 55
    Federation, as Act of, 59-61
    instability and change, 44
    locus of executive power, and, 72ff
    mechanism for change, 81
    preamble to, 61
    republic and, 27
    Senate, and, 73
    States and, 55
    written, 74, 91
    s 2, 61
    s 3, 61
    s 5, 61, 62
    s 6, 62
    s 9, 61
    s 17, 63
    s 28, 63
    s 35, 63
    s 51, 64
    s 52, 65
    s 53, 73
    s 57, 63
    ss 58-60, 100
    s 62, 73
    s 70, 100
    s 71, 64
    s 73, 64
    s 74, 59, 64
    s 75, 64
    s 90, 65, 66, 67, 68
    s 92, 76
    s 96, 69
    s 106, 62
    s 107, 62
    s 108, 62
    s 109, 62
    s 111, 65
    s 114, 66
    s 115, 66
    s 117, 66
    s 128, 81
    Ch II, 72, 74
    see also Commonwealth; Constitution, Imperial Parliament; Conventions; Bill of Rights; Parliament, Governor-General; Monarchy; States

Constitutional Monarchy, *see* Monarchy

Control, *see* Regulation

Conventions
    British Constitution and, the unwritten, 90, 91
    executive power and, exercise of, 74
    High Court and, if written into Constitution, 74
    see also Executive power; Responsible government

Corporations power, 65

Cultural change, 1, 6-8

Crown, the, 90ff, 96, 102, 103
    dismissal of government and, 94, 99ff
    legislature, as part of, 100
    parliament and, 92ff
    power of assent, 100
    see also Constitution; Monarchy

Cultural revolution, *see* Social change

Customs and excise, powers of, 65, 67
    see also Constitution, s 51; Taxation

Deakin, Alfred, 9

Democracy, 21

Demographics, 18ff
    see also Egalitarianism; Unemployment

Depression, 3
    see also Economic

INDEX

Diplomacy, regional, 141ff
    British interests, identification with, 142
    post-war period, 142
Discrimination, see Constitution, s 117; Gender roles
Dissident structures, 41
    see also Working class
Diversity, social and cultural, 51
    celebrating, importance of, 25
Dominant culture, 40
    see also Aboriginals
Dowling, Robert, 195
Drysdale, Russell, 7
Due process and entrenched rights, 76
Duties and excise, see Taxation; Customs and excise
Economic, 3-4, 44
    change, 15, 16, 19
    links with Asia, 23
    powers of Commonwealth parliament, 65, 67, 68, 70
    rationalism, 20
    regulation of and Constitution, 70, 71
    see also Constitution, s 51; Depression; Demographics; Taxation
Egalitarianism, 36
    Australian society and, 18
    social change and, 18, 19
    see also Working class
Empire,
    see Government, British
Employment, see Unemployment
England
    mother country, 24
    see also Government, British
Environmentalism, 20
    see also Regulation
Ethics, 21
Ethnic, 13
    see also Immigration
Europe, 45, 108
    centrism, 5, 8, 117
European Community and national redefinition, 26
Executive council, see Executive power; Governor-General
Executive power
    ministers, 72-73
    power to negotiate treaty and, 81

    Queen, vested in the, 100
    real nature of, 72
    see also Constitution; Governor-General; Prime Minister
Exile, see Alienation
Exportation, 66
    see also Constitution, federal powers; Economic
Family, 14, 70
    redefinition of, 15, 19
Federation, 3, 9, 12, 55, 59, 60, 61, 62, 88
    control of power and, 80
    federal executive power and, 63, 64, 65
    federal legislative power and, 64, 65
    State powers and, 64, 72
    see also Constitution
Feminism, 20
    see also Gender roles
Field, Barron, 6, 7, 8
Finances, see Taxation
    see also Constitution; Customs and excise; Economic
Foreign affairs, 9, 10
Foreign investment, 24
Free trade, between States, 66, 76
    see also Constitution, s 92
Freedom, 39
    desire for, 20
Friend, Donald, 199
Fundamentalism, see Regulation
Garnaut Report, 133
Gallipoli, 10
Gender roles, 4, 14, 16
    see also Social change
Generation, 5
Government, 55
    British, 9, 10, 101
    people in structures of, interest of, 88
    responsibility of, 94
    see also Responsible government
Governor-General, 9, 10, 63, 72, 73, 75, 91, 93, 99ff
    appointment by government and, 106
    British Government and, 87
    supply and, 75
    see also Constitution; Executive; Monarchy
Harpur, Royston, 200

INDEX

Head of State, 88ff, 97ff
   term of, 104
   see also Crown
High Court of Australia, 59, 64
   conventions of executive power and, 74
Home, 8
Hope, AD, 6
House of Representatives, *see* Constitution; Parliament; Senate
House of Review, *see* Senate
Hughes, Billy, 10
Human Rights, 127, 162ff
   individualism and, 127, 128
   see also Bill of Rights
Immigration, 22, 23, 45-47
   see also Multicultural; Multi racial
Imperialism, cultural, 174, 175
Income, changing patterns of distribution, 18, 19
India, 39-40, 44
   Australian literary imagination, in, 180
Individualism, 37
Indonesia, 125
Insecurity, national, 24
   see also Instability
Instability, social, 23
   see also Regulation
International and external affairs power, 71
   see also Commonwealth
International Treaty, *see* Treaty; Commonwealth
Ireland, President of, 107
Isaacs, Isaac, 10, 87
Japan, 115
   cultural difference to Australia, 37, 38
   emergence as economic power, 143
   process of national redefinition and, 26
Japonisme, 196
Jolley, Elizabeth, 8
Judiciary, 62, 64, 75
   Federal Court, 64
   High Court, 64
   policy/politics and, 75, 101
   see also Bill of Rights; Constitution, ss 71-75; Politics; Privy Council
Jurisdiction, *see* Judiciary

Keating, Paul, 4
Kerr, Sir John, 99, 104, 105, 161
Labor Party, 3
Land rights, 43
   see also Mabo
Lang, Premier, 94
Lawrence, DH, 7
Lawson, Henry, 11
Legislative, unlimited power, 101
   see also Commonwealth; Constitution, s 51; Parliament
Literature, 6-9
   Commonwealth, 5
   Australian and Asian, 169, 171ff
   Children's, 187
Litigation, extent of and Bill of Rights, 76
Lower House, *see* Senate
Mabo, 27, 28, 43
   cultural divide and, 43
   see also Aboriginals
Macaulay, Thomas Babington, 173
Mahoney, Dennis, 79
Malaysia, 124, 125
Male-dominated society, *see* Gender roles
Malouf, David, 8
Marginalisation, 49
   see also Working class
Marriage, *see* Family
McCaughey, Patrick, 7
McKinsey Report, 133
McMeekin, Ivan, 200
Media, Asian and Australian, 130, 135, 160
Menzies, Robert, 152
Middle class, 18
   see also Egalitarianism; Demographics
Migrants, 22, 37, 39, 45-47
   different roles of, 40
   see also Ethnic
Millenium, change and end of, 3
Ministers, *see* Executive power
Monarchy, 11, 22, 74, 87, 90-92, 97
   Head of State and international purposes, 88
   see also Crown; Executive power; Parliament, Queen and
Moorehouse, Frank, 8
Multi racial, 22

INDEX

Multicultural, 4, 22, 28, 29, 30-51, 102, 127
   see also Immigration; Nationalism; National identity; Migrants; Multi racial
Murray, Les, 8
Mutual understanding and trade relations, 158
Nation, birth of, 60
   see also Federation
Nation-state, 129
National identity, 1-30
   Arts and, the, 192
   see also Aboriginals; Asia; Immigration; Migrants; Social change; White Australia
Nationalism, 4, 11
   and identity, 45-46
New Australian, 25, 29, 45
   see also Ethnic
New Zealand, 57
   Bill of Rights, 77
   Constitution, provision for in, 58
Nolan, Sidney, 7
Olsen, John, 8
Opportunity, land of, 3, 15,
Orientalism, 175, 176, 193-195
   Asia as imperialist construct, 182
   see also Asian Studies
Overseas aid, 157ff
Parliament, 21, 92ff
   British Parliament and Constitution, 59, 60, 81, 82
   Commonwealth, 61, 62, 63, 72
   Governor-General and, no majority in, 74
   House of Representatives, 62, 63, 73
   Imperial Parliament, 9, 55, 58, legislative powers of Commonwealth, 64, 65
   Queen and, 62, 63, 92ff
   see also Constitution, s 51; Government; Responsible government; Senate; States; Sovereignty, parliamentary
Politics, 22
   Australian, 21
   judiciary and, 76
   major parties, 21
   see also Labor Party

Poverty, see Egalitarianism
Power, control of, 79
   and purpose of conferral, 80
Power, see Constitution
   see also Executive power
Preston, Margaret, 197, 198
Prime Minister, 72, 73, 74, 93, 96, 99
Privy Council, 10, 58
   abolition of appeals to, 27, 59, 64
   see Australia Acts
Productivity, 41, 42
   see also Economic
Proletariat, see Working class
Public Affairs Division, 133
Queen, see Monarchy
Racial Discrimination Act 1975 (Cth), 65
Racism
   Australian literature and, 178
   see also Xenophobia
Redistribution, see Egalitarianism
Referendum, 18, 82, 96
   see also Constitution, s 128
Regional headquarters, 136
Regional relations, 152ff
   pragmatism and, 155
Regulation, increase of, 20, 21
   see also Freedom
Reid, Sir George, 9
Religious tolerance, 134
Republic, 11, 22, 26, 83ff, 91ff, 97ff, 107
   debate, inadequate structure of, 41
   executive power and, 74
   interest in Asia, 150, 160ff
   members of Commonwealth and, 88
   minimalism and, 22, 26, 27, 89, 92, 97, 98ff, 105
   symbolism and, 27
   see also Constitution, change of
Reserve powers, 72ff
   see also Crown; Executive powers; Governor-General; Responsible government
Responsible government, 73, 92, 93, 99
   Constitution, not mentioned in, 100
   republican debate and, 98

INDEX

Responsible government *contd*
   see also Constitution; Executive power; Governor-General; Parliament; Westminster
Retrenchment, *see* Unemployment
Ross, Major Robert, 6
Rural identity, 24, 35, 45, 48
   see also Bush
Rushdie, Salman, 173
Said, Edward, 194
Scullin, James, 10, 87
Senate, 62, 63, 95
   republic and, 26
   supply and, 73, 75, 95
   term of senators, 63
   House of Representatives and, power of, 73
   see also Constitution; Parliament; States
Separation of Powers, 100, 101
Settler society and literature, 173
Singapore, 10, 127, 128
Social change, 14, 15, 18, 19
Social institutions, 15
   see also Family; Social change
Social unit, *see* Family
Socialism, 49
Sovereignty, 9-11
   parliamentary, 90, 92
   popular, 90
States
   Commonwealth and, relation between, 69, 71, 72
   federal power and, 64
   powers and Constitution, undefined, 71
   republic and, 26
   taxation powers and, 66-68
   see also Commonwealth; Constitution; Federation; Senate
Streeton, Arthur, 195
Supply, 100
   see also Constitution; Senate; Taxation
Supreme Courts, *see* Judiciary
   see also States
Taxation
   accountability, lack of, 69, 70
   sales tax, 67
   Senate and, 75
   States and, 67
   see also Constitution, s 51, s 90

Technology, and patterns of employment, 16
Trade Practices Act 1974 (Cth), 65
Trade, interstate, *see* Commonwealth; Constitution
Tradition, 41, 42
Tribalism, 41
Unemployment, 16, 17, 18
   see also Social change
Unions, importance for social cohesion, 50
United States, 142
   Constitution, 62
      Fifth Amendment, and role of judicial interpretation, 76
   culture, influence of, 24
   government and supply, 75
   national redefinition, 26
   system of government distinguished from Responsible government, 100
   wealth, patterns of distribution, 18
Upper House, *see* Senate
Urbanisation, 48
   high degree of, 25
   see also Bush
Values
   shared, 25
   Western, 127ff
Vietnam, 115, 124
Wealth, *see* Egalitarianism
Westminster, 9
   Statute of, 10
   system, 27, 75
   see also Constitution; Parliament
White Australia, 4, 28, 29
   policy of, 116, 148
   see also Mabo; Reconciliation
Whiteley, Brett, 8, 200
Whitlam Government, 94, 104
Williams, Fred, 8
Women, role of, *see* Gender roles
Work
   ethics, 17
   see also Unemployment
Working class, 41, 50
Working mother, 19
   see also Gender roles
Wright, Judith, 8
Writers, *see* Literature
Xenophobia, 117